Benjamin Scott

The contents and Teachings of the catacombs at Rome

Being a vindication of pure and primitive Christianity, and an exposure of the corruptions of

popery, derived from the sepulchral remains of the early Christians at Rome

Benjamin Scott

The contents and Teachings of the catacombs at Rome
Being a vindication of pure and primitive Christianity, and an exposure of the corruptions of popery, derived from the sepulchral remains of the early Christians at Rome

ISBN/EAN: 9783743414976

Manufactured in Europe, USA, Canada, Australia, Japa

Cover: Foto ©ninafisch / pixelio.de

Manufactured and distributed by brebook publishing software (www.brebook.com)

Benjamin Scott

The contents and Teachings of the catacombs at Rome

THE CONTENTS AND TEACHINGS

OF

THE CATACOMBS

AT

ROME:

BEING

A VINDICATION OF PURE AND PRIMITIVE CHRISTIANITY, AND AN EXPOSURE
OF THE CORRUPTIONS OF POPERY, DERIVED FROM THE

Sepulchral Remains of the Early Christians at Rome.

"Now I saw in my dream, that at the end of the valley lay blood, bones, ashes, and
mangled bodies of men ; . . . . and while I was musing what should be the
reason, I espied a little before me a cave, where two giants, POPE and PAGAN,
dwelt."—JOHN BUNYAN.

BY

BENJAMIN SCOTT, F.R.A.S.,

CHAMBERLAIN OF THE CITY OF LONDON, AND HONORARY SECRETARY OF
THE WORKING MEN'S EDUCATIONAL UNION.

Third Edition.

LONDON:
LONGMANS, GREEN, AND CO.
1873.

PRICE FOUR SHILLINGS.

GALLERIES OF THE CATACOMBS.

THE CONTENTS AND TEACHINGS

OF THE

CATACOMBS AT ROME.

DIAGRAMS

FOR THE USE OF LECTURES

HAVE BEEN PUBLISHED BY

The Working Men's Educational Union,

For the Illustration of the following Lectures;

THEY MAY BE OBTAINED OF

MR. W. THORN, 28, PATERNOSTER ROW, E.C.,

LONDON.

*** The Diagrams are 3 feet by 4 feet each, printed on cloth, coloured for gas-light, and are portable, effective, and durable. Price 3*s.* each.

In the following pages they are referred to thus [**74**]. Sketches of them will also be found there.

Illustrative of Pagan Practices.

Nos.

175. ASSYRIAN CRUELTY—Putting out eyes of Captives, etc. From the Ruins of Nineveh.

172. —————————Tongues torn out, etc. Ditto.

74. OFFERING CHILDREN TO MOLOCH.

75. DRUID SACRIFICE—(Described by Cæsar, *De Bell. Gall.* lib. vi. "Some have images of enormous size, the limbs of which they make of wicker-work, and fill with living men ; and, setting them on a fire, the men are destroyed by the flames. . . . . When there is not a sufficient number of criminals, they scruple not to inflict this torture on the innocent," etc., etc.)

76. CHILD-MURDER IN INDIA.

77. HINDOO SUTTEE ; or, Widow-burning on the Funeral Pyre of her Husband. The eldest son fires the pile.

78. THE DYING GLADIATOR.

The usual allowance to Subscribers and the Trade.

W. THORN, DEPOSITORY, 28, PATERNOSTER ROW.

PREFACE TO FIRST EDITION.

THE following pages contain the substance of four Lectures, delivered before an audience composed of working men; this statement will sufficiently account for their style. Gratified by the interest excited on their delivery, encouraged by several partial friends to give them a more enduring form, influenced by a knowledge that they were useful to some who heard them, and a hope that they may yet be serviceable to the class for whose benefit they were prepared, the writer has (amidst many distractions, arising from engagements of another character) committed them to the press.

He will be gratified if they shall in any degree serve to direct attention to a subject too much overlooked in this inquiring age—*the primitive condition of the Divine institution of Christianity*—particularly as exemplified by the inscriptions and works of early art in the Museums of Europe. Buried in ponderous and expensive folios, expressed in either foreign or dead languages, or locked up in the treasuries of distant antiquarian collections, the subject was inaccessible to the general reader, until the publication of the learned and deeply interesting work of Dr. Charles Maitland, "The Church in the Catacombs." Of the merits of that work it would be impertinent in the writer to speak. He may, however, be permitted to express the deep obligation under which he lies, as one of the public, for the pleasure and profit which it has afforded him ; he desires also gratefully to acknowledge the facilities which Dr. Maitland has kindly rendered in the preparation for the press of this little work, in which the writer has attempted to effect for the working-classes that which the Doctor has so admirably accomplished for the reading public in general. In every case in which "The Church in the Catacombs" has been quoted or referred to, the *second edition* has been used.

LONDON, *April,* 1860.

CONTENTS.

LECTURE I.

PAGANISM.

"The dark places of the earth are full of the habitations of
cruelty."—Psalm lxxiv. 20.

The subject of our present course of lectures introduces
us to the period called "the Augustan Age." This era,
commencing with the reign of Augustus Cæsar, born about
63 B.C., and comprising that of his immediate successors,
was greatly distinguished for the flourishing state of literature and learning, and the successful cultivation of the
fine arts.

Julius Cæsar, the great uncle and predecessor of
Augustus, had, by his victorious arms, rendered tributary
to Rome all the surrounding nations; and the Roman
Empire, on the accession of Augustus, was almost co-
extensive with the known world.

The religion of all these nations, with the single exception of the Jews, consisted of *Paganism*, in some form
or other, which was also the religion of Imperial Rome.
With her arms she had carried her gods, and promoted
their worship; or with politic tolerance, had adopted the
gods of other Pagan nations into her Pantheon. Farthest
India, Scythia, Southern Africa, and China, although un-
conquered, and consequently untributary to Rome, were
Pagan also. Notwithstanding the deities worshipped in
these countries differed in name, their attributes and

1

characters can be easily identified with those revered in the Roman Empire.

The Pagan system was *polytheistic*, that is, *many* gods were worshipped. These deities were generally represented under some human form, such as Jupiter, king of Olympus, and some score of other reprobates, whose names are doubtless familiar to you—Jupiter, Mars, Mercury, Neptune, Bacchus, Vulcan, Juno, Venus, and others, presiding over fighting, thieving, lust, debauchery, and drunkenness, with some few who personified domestic and civil virtues. These, together with deified kings, heroes, and freebooters, foreign gods, such as Isis of the Egyptians, and minor divinities or demigods, who presided specially over certain countries, cities, rivers, seasons, and groves, made up the list to hundreds, the "lords many and gods many," to whom homage was rendered by the civilized world at the period to which I allude.

Authors innumerable could be quoted to prove the number and the worthlessness of these divinities. One writer of the period satirically remarks, "it is easier to find a god than a man."* Livy, speaking of Athens, the chief city of Greece, says it was "full of the images of gods and men, adorned with every variety of material and with all the skill of art;"† while another writes, "on every side there are altars, victims, temples, and festivals." ‡ But not only did they worship every god whom they had invented, but in their feeling after a true God, "if haply they might find Him," conscious that there must be some one more worthy of their regard than the worthless creations of their own corrupt imaginings, they

* Petronius, Sat. xvii.   † Livy, 45, 27.
‡ Lucian Prometh., Book i. p. 180.

added to thousands of altars by erecting some to " *the Unknown God.*"

This fact is familiar to you from the statement in Luke's " Acts of the Apostles," which is fully confirmed by Pagan writers.* The Apostle Paul's spirit " was stirred within him when he saw the city" of Athens " full of idols" (Acts xvii. 16, *margin*); and in his address to the Athenian court of Arcopagus, he tells them, " I perceive that ye are altogether devoted to the worship of the gods, for as I passed hither and beheld your gods that ye worship, I found an altar with this inscription, To THE UNKNOWN GOD" (Acts xvii. 22, 23). As at Athens so was it at Rome, the world's capital, for we are told, on the authority of Minutius Felix, " they build altars to *unknown* divinities."

Such, then, was the polytheistic or pantheistic nature of the Pagan system, and now a few words upon the *character* of these gods, and the *nature of the worship* rendered to them ; and here I must premise that the subject forbids that I should be explicit. Suffice it to remark that there is no crime, however abominable, that was not imputed to them. In the words of Pope, their characters may be justly summed up—

> " Gods partial, changeful, passionate, unjust,
> Whose attributes were rage, revenge, and lust."

* Lucian, in his " Philopatris," uses the form of oath, " I swear by the *Unknown God* at Athens ;" and again he says (chap. xxix. 180), " we have found out the *Unknown God* at Athens, and worshipped him, with our hands stretched up to heaven." Philostratus says (in Vita Apollo, vi. 3), " and this at Athens, where there are even altars to the *unknown gods.*" Pausanius (in Attic., cap. 1) says that " at Athens there are altars of gods, which are called the *unknown ones.*" Diogenes Laertius mentions also these

As with the gods, so with the *system* with which they were identified, and its effects upon its votaries. I will judge that system out of the mouths of Pagans themselves. Aristotle* advises " that statues and paintings of the gods should exhibit no indecent scenes, *except* in the temples of such deities as preside over sensuality." What must have been the state of things to render such advice need-ful, and what the state of mind of an enlightened Pagan who could justify such an exception?

Petronius † informs us that temples were frequented, altars crowned, and prayers offered to the gods, in order that they might render agreeable unnatural lusts. The moral Seneca,† revolting at what he witnessed around him, exclaims, in the sight of such things, " How great is now the madness of men ! they lisp the most abominable prayers ; and if a man is found listening, they are silent ; *what a man ought not to hear, they do not blush to relate to the gods."* Again, " if any one considers what things they do, and to what they subject themselves, instead of decency, he will find indecency ; instead of the honourable, the unworthy ; instead of the rational, the insane." And to crown the testimony of Pagans as to the character and effects of their own system, Plato declares, " *man has sunk below the basest of the brutes."*

Well might the Apostle Paul, in writing to Rome at the very period to which I refer, paint the fearful picture contained in his first chapter of the Epistle to the Romans, which is fully borne out, as we have seen, by the testimony of Pagan writers. Well might he attribute it all to the

altars, and ascribes their origin to a period of pestilence (c.ted in Barnes' Notes, Acts xvii.)

* Politica, vii. 18, ed. Schneider.
† Cited in Tholuck's " Influence of Heathenism."

system of their religion, and the *character* of their gods, that they "changed the glory of the incorruptible God into an image made like to corruptible man, and to birds, and four-footed beasts, and creeping things; wherefore God also gave them up to uncleanness through the lusts of their own hearts." "And even as they did not like to retain God in their knowledge, God gave them over to a reprobate mind, to do those things which are not convenient; being filled with all unrighteousness, fornication, wickedness, covetousness, maliciousness; full of envy, murder, debate, deceit, malignity; whisperers, backbiters, haters of God, deceitful, proud, boasters, inventors of evil things, disobedient to parents, without understanding, covenant-breakers, without natural affection, implacable, unmerciful." * What a catalogue! It would have been sufficient for me to have quoted it, to have proved my point; but as there may be some among you who have not investigated the satisfactory evidence upon which the authenticity of the inspired writings rests, I have thought it best to place the combined testimony, Pagan and Christian, before you. Let me ask of you the favour that you will, at your leisure, read attentively the chapter from which I have quoted; it will assist you to appreciate a contrast which I shall have occasion to introduce in a subsequent lecture.

Respecting the character of ancient Pagan idols and idolatry beyond the bounds of the Roman Empire, we have not the same amount of information, but sufficient evidence exists to prove that oriental Paganism was equally degraded and degrading with that of Greece and Rome. Unchanged to the present hour, we can study it by actual observation; I will only quote one passage upon this point, from a public document laid before

* Rom. i. 23, 24, 28—31.

Parliament by a resident magistrate of Lower Bengal.* Speaking of the worship of the goddess Kalé, he says, " The murderer, the robber, and the prostitute, all aim to propitiate a being whose worship is obscenity, and who delights in the blood of man and beast, and without imploring whose aid no act of wickedness is committed."

There were, doubtless, exceptions to this rule. Some few of the gods personified virtues, and some men were found better than the system which prevailed; but these exceptions were rare indeed, and stand out upon the records of the times with a lustre the more brilliant in consequence of their infrequency. These men were virtuous, by reason of sparks of heavenly light not quite trampled out of their fallen nature; they were virtuous *in spite* of their religious system, and not *because of it.* Dionysius of Halicarnassus says, " There are *only a few* who have become masters of philosophy; on the other hand, the great and unphilosophic mass are accustomed to receive these narratives (the lives of the gods) rather in their worst sense, and to learn one of two things : either to despise the gods as beings who wallow in the grossest licentiousness, or not to restrain themselves even from what is most abominable and abandoned, when they see the gods do the same." †

Such, then, were the gods of Paganism; such the natural effects of their character upon their votaries.

* H. Oakley, Esq., cited in " Philosophy of Plan of Salvation."
† " It is absolutely impossible to write in detail of the shocking depravities of the old heathen world. The very rottenness of its sepulchre will ever most surely guard its own dreadful mystery. For it is a shame even to speak of those things which were done of them in secret. The reader need not be told how heavily charged with all kinds of moral death a religion must have been whose divinities were lechers, sots, fratricides, harlots, and panders;

I would next observe that the system of Paganism, like that of the Jews, was *sacerdotal*, that is, it was

its temples sacred brothels, the less scandalous alone of which could be tolerated within the walls of cities (Vitruvius, i. 7); its spectacles, the merciless gladiatorial shows, or scenes too impure for a soldierly Cato to witness; its processions, those of the Phallics; its altars not guiltless of human blood; its festivities, the Bacchanalia, the Saturnalia, the Floralia, the Cotyttia; its ritual vice, and its ministers of both sexes—but a veil must be thrown over their too warm devotion to their strictly sacerdotal functions. In the age of Augustus, marriage was rapidly growing into disuse, and had to be propped up by liberal bounties from the state. Where the tie existed at all, it was for the wife an indenture of servitude, she was the drudge; concubines and courtezans were the friends of her lord. Even this is the brighter side of the picture. There is not one of the odious vices for which the unclean Canaanites were doomed to extirpation, and the Cities of the Plain weltered in the fiery storm, which does not soil the portrait, handed down by history, of full many a ruler, statesman, poet, and philosopher of classic Greece and Rome. The fretting leprosy was everywhere. Few, indeed, of any rank in society escaped the plague, and the invention of monstrous pleasures was studied as a science, and followed as a thriving trade. Cruelty was as rampant as sensuality. Slavery was universal, and the dread power of life and death which the law gave to masters was sure to be no idle prerogative in the hands of men who gloated for days together over the dying throes of the gladiators."

"The aspirations of a Socrates were not those of the millions. The masses rather sought to gain the aid of their gods in the attainment of their, at best, animal and often devilish desires. They anointed, crowned, and kissed the images in which they saw and handled the divinities themselves; they regaled their nostrils with incense, and their appetites with the quivering limbs and smoking blood of the victims; they pledged them in cups of wine, whirled round them in frantic dances, or gashed themselves with knives, to coax or tease them to patronize some worldly scheme or other, even some filthy intrigue or murderous plot. In times of public calamity, the gods were dragged forth from the gloom of

administered by a priesthood—among the Pagans male
and female—who stood between the people and their
deities, offered their prayers, performed sacrifices, interpreted signs and omens, and communicated the will of
the gods, besides exercising certain judicial functions.

The worship consisted in the performance of certain
outward acts or rites ; was, in other words, exclusively
external or ceremonial : of preaching or the inculcation or
teaching of morals, *there does not exist a trace.** The
rites comprised sacrifices, offerings, prayers, burning
incense, pilgrimages to sacred places or shrines, processions in honour of the gods, abstinences, mortifications,
penances, observance of festivals, and frequently vicious
practices as above hinted.

These rites were costly, requiring a sacrifice on the
part of those who performed them, according to position
in life, and were suited to bestow more upon the rich
than upon the needy. They were not only sometimes
abominably impure, but oftentimes *barbarously cruel.*
Upon the impurity of the ceremonies it is impossible and
unlawful to speak ; nor would the statements be credited
when made, unless the authorities were cited at length.
Suffice it then to say, that whatever Christianity may or
may not have done, one of its effects is apparent ; it has
banished the general knowledge and even the names of
crimes then publicly committed, which not only reflected
no general discredit on those who practised them, but, as
the temples and laid on couches in the streets, that they might the
better see, and be moved by the tears of the whole population.
*Worship was manipulation, and prayer an exercise of the lungs, not
of the heart."*—" The Free Church of Ancient Christendom," by
Basil H. Cooper, B.A., pp. 31, 32, 20.

    * Vide Dr. Smith's " Dictionary of Antiquities," article *Sa-
cerdos.*

forming part of their religious rites, were in some cases obligatory, and in others accounted honourable and meritorious. It is a mercy the languages are dead in which such things are written ; but assuredly we do not well to forget the lessons which they teach.

I said the Pagan rites were often barbarously *cruel*. I referred chiefly to the practice of *offering human sacrifices*, which practice, so far as history has brought intelligence down to us, appears to have been universal. It is not known when this abomination was first introduced, but it was certainly very early in the world's history ; the Canaanites, more than 3300 years since, certainly practised it, offering their offspring to the idols of Canaan, to Moloch especially.* It was evidently one of the crimes assigned by the Almighty as the reason for the destruction of that people : " Thou shalt not let any of thy seed pass through the fire to Moloch. . . . . For all these abominations have the men of the land done, which were before you, and the land is defiled; that the land spue not you out also, when ye defile it, as it spued out the nations that were before you " (Lev. xviii. 21, 27, 28).

It may be needful to explain to some of you, that the expression in our Bibles, " to pass seed through the fire to Moloch," means to burn children to that divinity ; † upon this point no doubt exists. Moloch, Molec, Malcom, or Milcom, as he is variously called, was the planet Saturn deified, and his worship existed chiefly among the Canaanites, Ammonites, Carthaginians, and Phœnicians. He was represented by a statue of brass, under the form

* Deut. xviii. 9, 10.

† Compare Deut. xii. 31, xviii. 10 ; 2 Kings xvi. 3, etc., with Ps. cvi. 38 ; Jer. vii. 31, xix. 5 ; Ezek. xvi. 20, 21.

of a human being with the head of a bull; the arms of
the figure being extended forward, but declining towards
the earth; children were placed by their fathers in the
hands of the idol, and falling thence into a furnace
were burned to death; drums and trumpets drowning their cries. Sometimes the idol was hollow, and
heated to redness by fire placed within, in which
case the child was burned by the heated hand of the
figure. [**74.**]

In spite of the strongest prohibitions of this crime by
the Almighty, it was occasionally resorted to by the
Jewish kings and people, especially in the reigns of
Ahaz and Manasseh. The idol was erected in the valley
south of Jerusalem called Hinnom, but termed, in consequence of the practice of this abomination, *Tophet*, or
Drums, in reference to the drums beat to drown the cries
of the innocent victims.* The place became, consequently, so abhorrent to the more recent Jews that they
applied its name, Ge-hinnom, or Gehenna, to the place of
punishment in a future life. So that, in the estimation of
these Jews, it only required the practice of Pagan abominations to constitute a hell upon earth.†

And now let us pause for a minute while I extract a
lesson, in passing, from this Pagan superstition. I see
fathers and mothers present. I am a parent myself.
What think you, fathers, what say you, mothers,
could you bring yourselves to offer your children to
Moloch if you were living in Pagan times, and were
unvisited with the light of Christianity, received or
reflected ?

---

* 2 Kings xxiii. 10; Isa. xxx. 33; Jer. vii. 31, 32, xix. 4—14.

† Diodorus Sic., xx. 24; Eusebius Præp. Evang., iv. c. 16;
Jahn's Bib. Antiq , art. 410.

CHILDREN OFFERED TO MOLOCH.

74

DRUID SACRIFICE.

75

" A thousand voices answer ' No ! '
   Ye clasp your babes and kiss ;
   Your bosoms yearn, your tears o'erflow,
   Yet ah !—remember this :
   The infant trained alone for earth
   May live, may die, to curse its birth ;
   Is this a mother's love ?

" A parent's love may prove a snare ;
   The child she loved so well,
   Her hand may lead with gentlest care
   Down the smooth road to hell ;
   Nourish its frame, destroy its mind ;
   Thus do the blind mislead the blind,
   E'en with a mother's love."

The application will be apparent to you—the idolater of
old brought his child to the flames, and after a few
minutes of suffering, its spirit winged its flight to the
presence of its God. " Fear not," says the Saviour,
" those that kill the body, and after that have no more
that they can do." If we, by our neglect, by our counsel,
or (what is more influential than either) by our example,
destroy the souls of the children committed to us, how
will the comparison stand between ourselves and the
ignorant and inhuman votaries of Moloch, in that day,
when all alike, whatever their advantages or their disad-
vantages, must render an account of their stewardship ?

But I pass from this digression to consider further the
practice of offering human sacrifices. And first among
the civilized and philosophic Greeks. Agamemnon, king
of Mycene, offered up his daughter Iphigenia to obtain
a favourable wind to cross a sea not wider than the British
Channel, and a human sacrifice was offered again on his
return. The Athenians and Massalians annually offered
a man to Neptune. Menelaus, king of Sparta, being

detained by contrary winds, offered up two Egyptian children. History allows it to transpire, that many of the Grecian states offered human victims previously to undertaking an expedition or a war. At Rhodes, a man was offered to Chronos (agreeing with Moloch) on the 6th of July, annually; at Salamis, a man was offered in March, annually; at Chios and Tenedos, a human victim was annually torn in pieces. Erectheus sacrificed, in Attica, his daughter; Aristides sacrificed three nephews of the king of Persia; Themistocles sacrificed several noble persons. These men were not savages, bear in mind, but accounted wise, just, and benevolent in their day. In Thessaly, human sacrifices were offered; the Pelasgians, in a time of scarcity, offered *a tenth of their children;* in the Crimea, and among the Taurians, *every stranger* shipwrecked, instead of receiving the rights of hospitality, was sacrificed to Diana; her temple in Aricia was always served by a priest who had murdered his predecessor, and the Lacedemonians yearly offered her human victims, until the time of Lycurgus, who changed the custom into the sacrifice of flagellation, but boys were often whipped to death.

And to pass from the Greeks and their neighbours to Imperial Rome; history incidentally acquaints us with the fact that although probably less frequent, yet human sacrifices existed, and may be traced for many centuries. It was a custom to sacrifice annually thirty men, by throwing them into the Tiber, to obtain prosperity for the city. Livy mentions that two men and two women were buried alive to avert public calamities. Plutarch relates a similar sacrifice; and Caius Marius offered his daughter Calpurnia to ensure success in an expedition against the Cimbri. It is true a law was passed (B.C. 96) to put a stop to the practice, but this only proves that the custom existed. Besides which, the Pagan priest was oftentimes stronger than the civil magistrate, and the custom was not abolished although the law was promulgated, for numerous instances are mentioned, even as late as A.D. 300, nearly 400 years after the passing of the law.*

From Greece and Rome let us proceed to other nations of antiquity, and inquire what in this respect were the practices of Paganism.

Among the Tyrians the king frequently offered his son to procure prosperity; that this was the custom also among the Moabites, we gather from Scripture. In 2 Kings iii. 27, we read, on the occasion of the defeat of the king of Moab by the combined armies of Judah and Israel, "then he (king Mesha) took his eldest son, that should have reigned in his stead, and offered him for a burnt-offering on the wall." In New Testament times, Pilate mingled the blood of certain Galileans with his sacrifices. The Carthaginians followed the practice most extensively. On extraordinary occasions, *multitudes* of human victims were offered; thus, during a battle between the Sicilians and Carthaginians under Amilcar, the latter remained in the camp offering sacrifices to the deities of his country, and consuming upon one large pile the bodies of numerous victims.† Again, when Agathocles was about to besiege Carthage, its inhabitants, fearing that their misfortunes were attributable to the anger of Saturn, because they had offered him children of slaves and

* Vide Mühleisen's "Genuine and Spurious Religion," vol. ii. chap. iv.; and Horne's "Introduction to the Scriptures," vol. i. chap. i., notes.
† Herod., lib. vii. c. 167.

foreigners only, instead of noble children, sacrificed two hundred children of the best families to propitiate the offended deity, and three hundred citizens voluntary immolated themselves on the same occasion.* On another occasion, to celebrate a victory, the same people immolated all the handsomest of their captives, and the flame of the pile was so great that their camp was burned.† Tertullian, a Christian writer, says, that human sacrifices were common in Arcadia and at Carthage in his own day, even so recently as the third century of the Christian era.

And now to glance at the East. In Egypt, human victims were offered, and their ashes scattered over the land to procure fertility; red-haired men were selected. During the dynasty of the Hyksos, Manetho states, three were sacrificed daily, that is, over 1000 in a year; among the Persians we learn, incidentally, that the same practice prevailed. On the occasion of Annestris, the wife of Xerxes, reaching the age of fifty, fourteen children were buried alive as a thank-offering to the gods.‡ With respect to the Assyrians, we do not possess as yet sufficient information as to their mythology to say with certainty that human sacrifices formed a part of their religious system ; but the recent discoveries on the site of Nineveh, and the recovery of the written Assyrian language, by the exertions of Colonel Rawlinson, disclose the fact that gods were worshipped, to whom, in other countries, human victims

---

* Diodorus Sic., xx. c. 14.

† Ib. xx. c 65.

‡ Besides the authorities already cited, numerous testimonies, drawn from classic authors, may be found in Harwood's " Introduction to the New Testament," Bryant's " Analysis of Antient Mythology," and Dr. Leland's " Advantage and Necessity of the Christian Revelation."

172

ASSYRIAN CRUELTY. TONGUES TORN OUT. &c.

175

ASSYRIAN CRUELTY. EYES PUT OUT &c.

were offered.* That the Assyrians formed no exception
to the rule as regards the *cruelty* of Paganism, is evident,
as representations of flaying alive and other atrocious acts
of cruelty, form part of the decorations of their royal
palaces. [**172** and **175.**]

With regard to the Hindoos and Chinese, it will be
more satisfactory to quote their existing or recent practices,
as few of their ancient writings have come down to us.
Of the Hindoos, even under European sway, we find it
recorded in official documents—the public registers of
Bengal—that in the matter of widow-burning alone, between the years 1815 and 1824, that is in about ten years,
5997 widows were burned alive; and the cruelty is still
practised in parts beyond the influence of British rule.
Drowning and burying alive are also common. Among
the Chinese, children are, in Tunquin, sacrificed by cutting
in two or by poison; and in Laos, on founding a temple,
the work is cemented by the blood of the first stranger
who passes. Children are also thrown into the rivers, as
sacrifices to the water.

To come nearer home, let us inquire concerning the
practice among the Pagans of northern Europe. Materials
are scarce from which to ascertain facts, but from these
abundant evidence of the practice, in all its malignity,
may be elicited. Harold, the Saxon king, slew two of
his sons in order to obtain a storm to wreck the fleet of
the Danes. In Russia, as late as the tenth century, a
man was chosen by lot and sacrificed to appease the anger

* Rawlinson's "Outlines of History of Assyria." The same
researches disclose that the worship of the goddess Milytta prevailed, whose rites consisted of revolting obscenity. The same
mark applies to Babylon.

of the gods. In Zealand, ninety-nine persons were annually sacrificed to the god Swan-to-wite ; in Denmark, the same number of men, horses, cocks, and hawks. The Scandinavians sacrificed every captive to Odin. The Slavonian priests not only slew human victims, but drank their blood. The mode of destroying life differed, but the principle was the same, and appears to have been universal. The Galli killed with the stroke of an axe, so administered as not to deprive immediately of life, but to obtain convulsions in the victim by means of which omens could be obtained ; the Celts laid their victims on an altar, and opened the breast with a sword ; the Cimbri ripped up the bowels ; the Norwegians knocked out the brains with the yoke of an ox ; the Icelanders pierced the victim with arrows. In Britain, a wicker figure in the human form was filled with victims and burned.* [75.]

The details are not only revolting but, I fear, wearisome. I cannot, however, consider this part of the subject complete without glancing at countries which may be classed with those of antiquity, notwithstanding almost nothing is known of their ancient history, for their religion is now, or was until very recently, in every sense Pagan, and it is safe to conclude it was the same at the period to which I more particularly refer. I allude chiefly to the continents of America, Africa, and the islands of the Pacific. In Mexico, the crime of sacrificing human victims appears to have reached its utmost development; no author estimates the number of the victims annually at less than 20,000, and some carry the number as high as 50,000. On great occasions the number slaughtered became really appalling. At the dedication of the great temple Huitzilo-polchli, in the

* Mühleisen, vol. ii. chap. 4.

year 1486, the prisoners, who had been long reserved for the purpose, ranged in files, formed a procession nearly two miles in length; the ceremony lasted several days, and 70,000 are said to have perished. The companions of Cortez, the conqueror of Mexico, counted 136,000 skulls at one of their temples. When Montezuma, the last emperor of Mexico, was asked why he had suffered the republic of Tlascala to maintain her independence, he replied, "That she might furnish me with victims for the gods."* On the occasions of seasons of drought, to propitiate Theloc, the god of rain, children were sacrificed, dressed in fine robes, decked with the early blossoms of the spring. As they were carried along in litters to the place of slaughter, writers state that the cries of these innocents would have moved the hardest hearts. Not so! they could not affect the hard hearts of the Pagan priests, who, like the votaries of Moloch, drowned their cries with noisy music and chanting. To crown the picture, these innocent victims were generally bought by the priests from their *poor parents;* and parents were found to sell their offspring. This was also the case with ancient Paganism.†
" Without natural affections" is indeed the true verdict of the inspired Apostle before referred to. But I must be brief in my remaining review of Pagan cruelty. The Fantih, and many other tribes of Africa, offer human sacrifices every new moon. In Ashantee, the worship of sharks and snakes is accompanied by human sacrifices in their most appalling forms.‡ The late king of Ashantee gave directions for the slaughter of 6000 slaves at his funeral, which hideous testament was put in execution. In every

* Prescott's " Conquest of Mexico."
† Mühleisen's " Genuine and Spurious Religion," vol. ii. p. 209.
‡ Hutchinson's " Western Africa."

discovered island of the Pacific the practice was found to prevail. At Otaheite, appalling numbers were slaughtered: the eye of the victim being first taken out to present to the king. At the Marquesas Islands, among the inhabitants of Palliser's and Harvey Islands, and of New Zealand, they not only sacrificed their enemies, *but devoured them.*

It forms no part of my plan in this course of lectures to enter upon the inquiry, how the offering of sacrifices, and particularly human sacrifices, became universal. Suffice it to remark, in passing, that there is scarcely any practice of Paganism but may be traced to some foundation of truth. Thus sacrifices, whether offered by the Jews or the Pagans, recognized three great truths : firstly, that man had offended his God; secondly, that some atonement must be offered, or recompense made to satisfy offended law ; and, thirdly, that a vicarious atonement would suffice, that is, an innocent victim would be accepted in the place of the sinner himself. These ideas appear to have existed universally ; there is hardly a corner of the world in which they cannot be traced. They doubtless originated in the Divine communication made to man, in the earliest state of his existence, as to the method which had been devised for effecting reconciliation between fallen man and his offended Maker. The truth became corrupted, but conscience, by arousing incessantly man's guilty fears, prevented its being entirely lost. Feeling his need of a costly offering, and losing sight of the most costly of all offerings which God had engaged to provide, man sought in the sacrifice of human life, which all value so highly, to provide an offering adequate to his guilt ; and thus arose a practice of sacrificing " the fruit of the body for the sin of the soul." It is not, however, the origin of Pagan ideas, but the state of the Pagan world which is the subject of our lecture.

I must now inquire, very briefly, if such were the religious rites, what was the SOCIAL AND MORAL CONDITION of Pagans at the period under review?

The voice of history, fairly listened to, making all allowances for poetical hyperbole and philosophical misrepresentations, asserts most unequivocally that the social condition of the people was wretched and degraded in the extreme.

Infanticide, the practice of destroying young children, prevailed almost as universally as those practices to which I have just alluded. Not in barbarous countries only, where it is still prevalent, such as India and China, and among some of the American tribes—where the digging of the grave by the mother precedes the birth of her child—but I refer again to polished Greece and civilized Rome.

Among the Athenians and Gauls, the laws authorized parents to destroy their children. At Sparta, the laws of Lycurgus required the father to bring the child before an examining committee, and if found deformed or weakly, it was cast into a deep cavern near Mount Taygetus. Aristotle says, " it is necessary to expose (that is, to leave to perish) weak and sickly children, to prevent too rapid an increase of citizens." Plato, in his " Model Republic," provides that children likely to prove weakly should not see the light. So at Rome, the laws of Romulus gave parents authority to put their children to death. Erixo and Arius, Roman citizens, each flogged his son until he

expired.*   Tertullian affirms " they exposed their sons,
drowned them, or allowed them to perish by famine or by
dogs." Cicero and Seneca both speak of the practice
incidentally, but treat it as a matter of course, without
censure or even without comment. Terence describes one
Chremes as " a man of universal benevolence," but nevertheless represents him as commanding his wife to expose
her new-born infant, and flying into a passion with her
for committing the painful and unnatural duty to another.†

* Seneca, de Clem., i., 4, 15.

† Vide Mühleisen, ii. chap. 4; also a paper in the " Leisure
Hour," No. 8, 1852.

Child murder, particularly female infanticide, is thus referred
to by a modern writer, Thomas Bacon, Esq., F.S.A., author of "First
Impressions and Studies from Nature in Hindustan," in a paper
on Benares, in the " Oriental Annual," 1839, pp. 92—94:—
" The revolting crime of infanticide was at one time carried to a
great height in Benares and the adjacent districts; and there can
be little doubt, by the account of the Mussulmans, that it is still
occasionally practised, in defiance of the active measures for its
prevention adopted by the Government. . . . . The great
supporters of this iniquitous practice were formerly the Rajh-
poots, the Rajhkomars, and the Rajhvansis, among whom a single
female infant was never permitted to exist; nor did they consider
their destruction as an act of sin or cruelty, though I am unable
to believe, as many have affirmed, that they regard the sacrifice as
an acceptable offering to the gods. It appears rather to have
originated in convenience, on account of the ruinous expense
attending their marriage, and to have been practised without fear
of offence to the deities, for their belief is, that the souls of those
daughters who were thus destroyed were eventually returned to
them in the persons of sons; and when this did not appear to be
borne out by the birth of a male child, it only followed that Siva
was displeased, and conciliation was resorted to, until a son should
really be born to them. In these cases it was usual to seek pro-
pitiation by placing the next female infant in the hands of the

I cannot leave this subject without quoting the testimony of a writer, which will be the more valuable, as he strove to paint heathenism in bright colours at the expense of Christianity. Gibbon writes thus : " The exposure of children was the *stubborn and prevailing vice of antiquity* ; it was sometimes prescribed, often permitted, almost always practised with impunity, even by nations who

Brahmins, to be solemnly sacrificed in the temple of the Genesa, whereby that god might be moved to compassion for the babe and be induced to intercede with Siva for the future birth of male children to the parents. It is easy to perceive whence this delusion had its commencement, since a handsome douceur to the immolating priests was an indispensable part of the ceremony, which in all respects differed from the method of destruction privately used. In the latter place the operation was performed with very little form or expense, by what the Hindoos call *drinking milk*. No sooner had the sex of the infant been ascertained, than a caldron of warm milk was brought into the apartment where the mother lay, and after prayers for the child's return in the form of a son, the little innocent was immersed in the milk, and held down until life became extinct, and then it was carried to the Ganges and thrown into the stream. When, however, the deed was committed to the Brahmins to be executed by way of sacrifice to Genesa, the poor babe was carried to the temple, and, being laid upon its back, was, after certain diabolical ceremonies, destroyed by the club of the inhuman *fakir*." [76.]

The Rev. T. H. Horne, in his admirable and learned work, " Introduction to the Study of the Holy Scriptures," states that "*not fewer than ten thousand children are computed to be thus murdered (i.e.,* by abortion or after birth), *in the single province of Bengal, every month*" (vol. i. p. 18). Speaking of China, he says : " Polygamy universally prevails, as also the cruel practice of exposing infants to perish ; not fewer than *nine thousand* of whom are computed to be annually destroyed at Pekin, and the same number in the rest of the empire " (vol. i. p. 19). See authorities referred to in that work for these statements.

never entertained the Roman ideas of paternal power; and the dramatic poets, who appeal to the human heart, represent with indifference a popular custom which was palliated by the motives of economy and compassion." *

Let us next inquire what was the *social condition of the female sex.*

* Gibbon, in his "Decline and Fall of the Roman Empire," thus writes of the *condition of children* under the Roman laws:—"In his father's house he (the son) was a mere *thing;* confounded by the laws with the moveables, the cattle, and the slaves, whom the capricious master might alienate or destroy, *without being responsible to any earthly tribunal* (chap. xliv. p. 367). According to his discretion, a father might chastise the real or imaginary faults of his children by stripes, by imprisonment, by exile, by sending them to work in chains among the meanest of his servants. The majesty of the parent was armed with the power of life and death, and the examples of such bloody executions, which are *sometimes praised and never punished,* may be traced in the annals of Rome beyond the times of Pompey and Augustus" (chap. xliv. p. 368). Such is the testimony of an enemy to Christianity to the cruelty of Paganism; now mark his undesigned testimony to the ameliorating and humanizing nature of Christianity in these respects:— "The Roman Empire was *stained with the blood of infants,* till such murders were included by Valentinian and his colleagues in the letter and spirit of the Cornelian Law" (chap. xliv. p. 371). This was about the year A.D. 438, after the triumph of Christianity, *temp.* Valentinian III.

An illustration of the *treatment of children,* at the height of Rome's civilization, may be found in the case of the execution of Sejanus, *temp.* Tiberius. His children, a boy and girl, too young to partake of his guilt, were condemned to death with him. The girl, with infantine simplicity, asked what she had done, and promised never to do it again, but neither youth, sex, nor innocence could shield her; in compliance with a *vile custom,* she was first ravished, then put to death. The bodies of both children, being dragged through the streets, were cast into the Tiber.—See Ferguson's " Roman Republic," vol. v. p. 354.

Woman was everywhere considered as inferior to man. In Hindostan, in China [76], and in the South Seas, female infants are still destroyed for this reason. In northern Bengal, *female* infants are suspended in baskets to the branches of trees, and perish by ants, flies, and birds of prey. So much for the female sex in infancy; but in after years, if she survived, woman was degraded to the lowest level. Aristotle writes, "Women are a kind of monsters—the beginning of degeneracy of our nature."

Polygamy, that is, the practice of having many wives at the same time, although forbidden by the laws of some countries, was nevertheless universally prevalent. I need not point out to you that this practice is evidently contrary to nature, which provides an almost absolute equality of the sexes. Neither need I say that it is a practice peculiarly degrading to woman, treating her as if she were incapable of the affectionate attachment which so distinguishes her sex; affording her no opportunity of centering her affections upon one object, furnishing her, at best, with a divided heart.

Woman was defined by the laws of Rome, *not as a person but as a thing*, and if the title to her were wanting, she could be claimed like other moveables * She was treated as the slave of man, not his helpmate, companion, and best friend ; was bought, sold, exchanged, betrothed, married, divorced, and separated from her children, without consent, often without mercy, as suited the caprice of her master—I cannot term him her husband; who could lawfully put her to death, even for sipping his wine or using his keys.†

* Gibbon's " Decline and Fall," chap. 44, p. 373.
† Pliu. Nat. Hist., xiv. 14; Plutarcb, p. 57.

It may not be unprofitable to listen to the living testimony of one who has witnessed the condition of woman under the influence of *modern* Paganism.* " Truly," he says, "the life of an Indian female, from the cradle to the grave, is one of misery. Have we not heard the melancholy tale of the little one betrothed in early childhood to one who feels no interest in her, and on whom she looks only with awe ; from her wedding-day compelled to live a poor, down-hearted, abject slave ; waiting on her lord in silent and submissive servitude, performing every menial office without one syllable of thanks or comfort; and on that awful day when death removes her tyrant, compelled *to burn with him*, a living holocaust, *or to sit down beside him in the tomb whilst the earth covers them above.*† [**77.**]

" Or, again : have we not heard of India's daughters in the south, casting aside the feelings and tenderness of womanhood, and acting the Pey-adi in their demon-worship, with all its horrible accompaniments, *drinking the life-blood of the slaughtered victim* even to intoxication, and whirling round in her unnatural frenzy till she sinks exhausted on the ground—herself the victim of her own

---

* Dr. Vidal's Sermon for the Society for Promoting Female Education in the East.

† " Between the years 1815—1820 there came under the notice of the Bengal Government the cases of no less than 62 *girls* under the age of eighteen, who were thus cruelly destroyed. The ages of these poor girls were as follows :—14 were seventeen years old ; 1 was sixteen and a half years ; 22 were sixteen years ; 6 were fifteen years ; 2 were fourteen years ; 2 were thirteen years ; 10 were twelve years ; 1 was ten years ; 3 were only eight years of age." (" The Pioneers, or Early Christian Missionaries of Bengal." G. Gogerly.) This barbarous custom of Suttee was abolished by Lord William Bentinck in 1830.

CHILD OFFERED TO GENESA.

HINDOO SUTTEE.

wild and terrible imaginings and of that evil spirit to which she has devoted herself? When questioned as to the prospect of her soul, her vacant answer is, ' My soul, my mother? *What soul have I? I am a woman; no, my mother, no; I am but a woman.'* "

" Once more : let us direct our eyes more eastward, to the teeming multitudes of China, that land of dwarfed and stunted promise; how is it with the female there ? Oh ! what a tale of woe does that single fact reveal, which meets us on the very threshold, which stares us in the face the moment we set foot upon her shores ; I mean the prevalence of horrible infanticide, by which the female infant is consigned to death as soon as born, murdered without compunction, as the almost unavoidable necessity attaching to its sex. *Where it is accounted a disgrace and a misfortune to be the father of a female child*—where two such children out of every four fall victims to this terrible delusion, what can we expect with reference to the lot of the survivors ? Thus debased, despised, counted unfit to live, a disgrace and reproach to the family of which she ought to be the ornament and honour, the *Chinese* female may be well described as joining her lament to those of her *Mahometan* and *Indian* sisters. ' Is it nothing to you, all ye that pass by ? Behold, and see if there be any sorrow like unto my sorrow, which is done unto me.' "

I could weary you with tales of cruelty and of bloodshed, arising from the Pagan view of the social position of woman. But enough has been said, I trust, to satisfy you that *woman*, at least, has been a gainer wherever she has escaped from the influence of Paganism. But you may imagine that, as I have dwelt upon the misery of childhood and womanhood under Paganism, I have little to say concerning the social and moral condition of society generally.

In every picture there are points which first arrest our attention, from the strength with which they stand out from the canvas. It is so with regard to the picture which history and literature have left of the times when Paganism was everywhere triumphant. As we begin to read, we are struck by *isolated* acts of cruelty or injustice towards certain classes, and particularly towards the helpless; continuing to peruse and to reflect, we are impressed with the *general* depravity, misery, and degradation of the whole of society, from the emperor to the slave; and reasoning upon the matter, we arrive at the certain conclusion that, had not all ranks and classes and both sexes been alike degraded, a loud, indignant protest from some class must have been heard rising above the wails of misery and the frenzied shouts of their bacchanalian orgies.

But you will require something in the shape of facts, to enable you to come to a verdict upon this statement. I will furnish you with a few illustrations, gathered from a field which would yield a plentiful crop of like baneful testimonies; first, referring to the rulers and governors, then to the common people or freemen, and, lastly to the slaves.

The histories of the lives of the *Roman emperors, their families, and connections*, with few and therefore remarkable exceptions, exhibit all the vices of which fallen nature is capable; could their biography be written in the Newgate Calendar of our day, it would blacken its pages. As these emperors were frequently raised to the imperial purple by the voice of popular election, or that voice ratified and confirmed their appointment, it will be

obvious that they reflect the social condition of the masses
who assisted them to rank and dignity. Not to appear
invidious in making a selection, I will briefly enumerate
the crimes attributed to a few of the first and greatest of
the Cæsars.

Julius Cæsar, the successful soldier and talented
general, slew in war, mostly waged for the advancement
of himself and the gratification of his inordinate ambition,
upwards of *eleven hundred thousand men*,* and corrupted,
according to the statement of a talented Frenchman who
has reviewed his life, one half of the ladies of rank and
influence at Rome. " Cæsar," says he, " who destroyed
the agents of his crimes if they failed in address ; Cæsar,
the husband of every wife, ... has
been accounted a great man by the mob of writers ; the
talents of this singular man, and the good fortune which
constantly attended him till the moment of his assassination, have concealed the enormity of his actions." †

Augustus, one of the *best* of the emperors, was guilty
of heartless adultery and gross licentiousness ; his only
daughter, Julia, became infamous for her abandoned conduct, for which she was banished by her father, to the
influence of whose example her corrupt actions must be
attributed.

Tiberius, who succeeded Augustus, was a monster of
cruelty, intemperance, and debauchery. " Not only his
relations and friends, but the great and opulent were
sacrificed to his ambition, cruelty, and avarice ; and there
was scarcely in Rome one single family that did not reproach him for the loss of a brother, a father, or a
husband. He at last retired to the island of Capreæ, on

* Platt's " Universal Biography," vol. i. p. 651.
† M. Ophellot, " Mélanges Philosophiques."

the coast of Campania, where he buried himself in unlawful pleasures. In his solitary retreat he proposed
rewards to such as invented new pleasures, or could produce luxuries. He disgraced himself by the most unnatural vices and enormous indulgences, which can draw
a blush even upon the countenance of the most de-
bauched and abandoned."* His intemperance was such,
that it was wittily observed by Seneca, "that he was
never intoxicated but once in his life, for he continued in
a perpetual state of drunkenness from the time he gave
himself up to drinking until the last moment of his existence."

Yet Tiberius, with his predecessors Julius and
Augustus, and many of their successors, were, after
death, *raised to the rank of gods, and worshipped as
divinities at Rome.* If such were thy gods, Roman citizens, what must have been the condition of yourselves ?

Caligula, next in succession, committed the most atrocious acts of impiety, cruelty, and folly. He began his
career of wickedness by murdering several of his relations, senators, and people of rank. He openly married
his own sister Drusilla, and on her death caused divine
honours to be paid in temples built to her. For his
favourite horse he erected a palace, with a marble stable
and ivory rack, and fed him with gilt barley out of a
golden cup. He introduced his said horse to the temple
in the vestments of the priest of Jupiter, and caused
sacrifices to be offered to himself, his wife, and his steed.
He married several wives, whom he put away one after
another. Cruelty became in him an inordinate habit; he
gave directions for a murder on one occasion, in these

* Platt's "Universal Biography," vol. i. pp. 709—711.

words, " Strike in such a manner *that he may feel himself die.*" On another occasion he exclaimed, " Would to heaven that the Roman people had but one head, that it might be struck off at a blow !" He seems, as Seneca observes, " to have been brought forth by nature for the express purpose of showing how much mischief could be effected by the greatest depravity, supported by the highest power."*

Claudius, apparently by nature of a weak and inoffensive turn of mind, commenced his reign so as, in some degree, to redeem the character of his class, and to win the respect of the Roman people ; but his wife Messalina supplies us with an illustration of the social and moral condition of the high-born at that period, which might be considered as wanting in the person of the emperor. Her name has become infamous in relation to all that is abandoned in her sex ; she was no less notorious for cruelty, which her influence over the emperor enabled her to perpetrate in his name. It would be tedious to enumerate all her acts, suffice it to state the members of his own family whose deaths she procured : Appius Silanus, who married the emperor's mother-in-law, Silanus and Pompey, his sons-in-law, and his two nieces, the Livias. Suetonius, also informs us, that thirty-five senators and above three hundred knights were executed by Claudius. The most extraordinary event in his reign was the *public marriage* of Messalina, the empress, to a young noble named Silius, during the temporary absence of the emperor at the sea-coast. That abandoned woman, not content with the most undisguised display of her fondness for her paramour, had

* Platt's " Universal Biography," vol. ii. p. 10.

resolved to show her contempt for all ordinary decency by this step; they were married in sight of the whole city, with all the accustomed nuptial ceremonies. What must have been the moral condition of the people who could, complacently and without excitement to riot, witness such conduct in high places? Messalina having been put to death, the emperor married his niece, who endeavoured to emulate Messalina's conduct, and eventually poisoned her imperial husband.*

Nero succeeded Claudius, and most appropriately closes my catalogue. He appears to have attained an eminence in all that is disgraceful to human nature, which has never been surpassed. He frequented, nightly, in disguise, all the scenes of debauchery which Rome contained, acted publicly at the theatre, contended in a state of nudity at the public games, and before the assembled people displayed the most abominable conduct which it is possible to conceive, and is impossible to describe. He caused Rome to be set on fire in different places, and during several days enjoyed the dreadful scene to which his atrocious barbarity had given rise, playing upon a lyre on the top of his palace, and singing the destruction of Troy. To crown all, this monster having failed in a deliberately-planned scheme for drowning his own mother, caused her to be assassinated.†

Such were the first emperors of Rome; were I to continue the scrutiny further it would but weary and disgust, and the result would be generally the same. Although a Titus, a Nerva, or a Trajan happily arise at intervals to vary the history, yet a Domitian, insisting

* Platt's "Universal Biography," vol. ii. p. 4.

† Platt's "Universal Biography," vol. i. p. 717, etc.; vol. ii. pp. 10—12.

upon being styled "God," but addicted to incest and killing flies; a Commodus, who dishonoured all his sisters, and cut off the noses of his courtiers under pretence of shaving them; a Caracalla, who murdered his wife and his own brother in his mother's arms; and a Heliogabalus, who chose a senate of abandoned women, and exalted his horse to the dignity of the consulate, but too completely confirm my statements regarding the moral and social condition of those who bore rule in Rome.

The general condition of society may be gathered from what has preceded. The Romans, as a people, must have been strangely corrupted, to have been incapable of protecting themselves from such detestable vice and tyranny, practised by so many of their emperors; extreme degeneracy of the people must have deprived them of all right principles, morals, and sentiments, before such excesses of absolute power could have taken place. If there be anything of generous and masculine public opinion exhibited, it has been generally found sufficient to make the laws of society and the requirements of decency respected, even in states not so free as was ancient Rome.

The moral state of a populace may be conveniently estimated by the mode in which the hours of relaxation are spent, and by the character of the amusement suited to the popular taste. In this respect history affords abundant evidence of the degraded morals of the Roman people. Their amusements consisted chiefly of public games, carried forward in their spacious amphitheatres, which were almost invariably accompanied either by gross indecency or by frightful cruelty and waste of life. With respect to the first class of representations, it will be sufficient to state that riots on more than one occasion took place, when, out of respect to common decency, reformation of this abuse was attempted.

A few words on their *cruel sports*, and particularly the *gladiatorial combats*, will not be uninstructive.

In the earliest records the practice of slaying domestic animals, captives, or slaves at the tombs of departed kings and chieftains may be traced, and it appears to have existed in many nations widely separated from one another. Indeed, to the present day the practice prevails among many of the American-Indian and African tribes, and numerous examples might be cited from the funereal rites with which Achilles honoured the pyre of his friend Patroclus, and the funereal pile of the king of Assyria, mentioned by Diodorus, on which all the king's wives were burned, to that of the Hindoo suttee, and the burial of the mother of the king of Ashantee in 1817, when three thousand human beings were immolated.

The practice, however, was so congenial to the tastes of a cruel populace, that it became a matter of *amusement*, and these games were common at Rome, even in the period of the republic; while under the emperors they assumed a magnitude which astonishes and almost passes belief.

They consisted of contests waged between brute beasts, or between men and wild beasts, and gladiatorial combats between man and man. Various buildings were set apart for these cruel exhibitions; and the Flavian Amphitheatre, now known as the Colosseum, the largest building the world has seen, capable of seating a hundred thousand persons, was specially dedicated to this fiendish sport.

And first with respect to the *animal combats*, it is astonishing to read of the number of animals wantonly excited against one another and slain. As early as the year 251 B.C., the slaughter of one hundred and forty-two elephants in the circus is mentioned.* In the year 168 B.C., sixty-three panthers, and forty bears and elephants made sport for the Romans ;† from this time combats between elephants and lions, lions and bulls, bears and elephants, etc., recur so frequently, that it would be tedious to recite the instances. The evil, however, increased in magnitude as the empire advanced, as may be gathered from the almost incredible number of animals said to have been slaughtered. A hundred lions were exhibited by Sulla and destroyed by javelin-men.‡ At games given by Pompey, B.C. 55, immense numbers were put to death, among which are mentioned six hundred lions and twenty elephants. Julius Cæsar, in his third consulship, B.C. 45, gave an entertainment of the kind, which lasted five days, in which giraffes were first introduced, and men from Thessaly combated with infuriated bulls. The hippopotamus, rhinoceros, crocodile, and rattle-snake were introduced by subsequent emperors to vary the sport. At the consecration of the grand amphitheatre of Titus, *five thousand* wild beasts and *four thousand* tame animals were killed ;§ while Trajan, celebrated among Roman emperors for his clemency, on the occasion of a victory over the Dacians, slaughtered as many as *eleven thousand* animals in the rejoicings which followed.||

* Pliny, Nat. Hist., viii. 6. † Livy, xxxix. 18.
‡ Seneca de Brev. Vit. 13. § Suet. *Tit.* 7 ; Dion. Cass., lv. 25.
|| Dion. Cass., lxvii. 15.

3

But the half has not been told; numerous as were the animals put to death in these games, they were as nothing compared with the multitudes of *human beings* who were slaughtered in cold blood to satisfy the unnatural and depraved craving for scenes of bloodshed and cruelty. Passing over all reference to those who fell in the combats with wild animals, I proceed to consider the gladiatorial combats, conducted solely by men. [78, 79.] The combatants were generally captives taken in war, slaves, or condemned criminals, though frequently free-born citizens entered the lists for hire.

"As they fight," says a modern writer, "the spectators narrowly and eagerly watch each blow; when one is wounded, the exulting cry, '*Habet, habet*' (he has it, he has it), rings through the amphitheatre. If the wound be so severe as to disable him, he lowers his arms in token of defeat; then, raising his hand, looks up to the people with mute, imploring gaze, asking them to spare his life. If he has acquitted himself very well, or has in any way won the favour of the spectators, his request may perhaps be granted; but when their passions and thirst for blood have been excited, or if he have shown any signs of fear, his death is inevitable. The people give the well-known fatal signal by turning up their thumbs. As he rolls his dim, despairing eyes along the crowded benches, and meets only the merciless gaze of men and women, from whose hearts every vestige of pity has been effaced, he yields himself to his fate. The conqueror plunges his sword into the breast of his old companion; the blood gushes forth and dyes the sand; the attendants come in, strike a hook into the mangled corpse, drag it out, strew fresh sand or sawdust over the spot; a shower of perfumed waters refreshes the specta-

78

79

tators; the bets which have been won or lost are settled, and then the sports begin again; and the same scene is repeated through the whole day, and often for many days in succession. Sometimes, to render the sports more attractive, the *libelli* (handbills) announced that they would be '*sine missione*,' that is, that no defeated gladiator would be spared." Lipsius, the great authority on this question, reckons that the combats of the amphitheatre cost from _twenty to thirty thousand lives per month,_ and adds, that no war ever waged has caused so much slaughter as these games. When we reflect that the throng of eager spectators included all classes, from the emperor to the meanest slave—the knight, the senator, the priest, the matron, the vestal virgin—all the pomp and refinement with all the rudeness and brutality of the empire—swelled the crowd which flocked to glut its eyes with blood, and to exult in the cries and groans of the wounded and the dying—we shall feel no difficulty in estimating the *moral, condition* of the people under the influence of Paganism in the refined and civilized Augustan age.*

The limits of a single lecture render it impossible to allude to all the evils resulting from the Pagan system; the following illustrations of *moral depravity* may be, however, adduced.† *Profane swearing* was commended, if not by the precepts, yet by the example of the best heathen moralists—particularly Socrates, Plato, and Seneca, in whose works numerous oaths occur. Many of them not only pleaded for *self-murder*, as Cicero, Seneca,

* Vide Smith's "Dictionary of Roman and Greek Antiquities," articles *Venatio, Bestiarii,* and *Gladiatores,* and a paper in the *Leisure Hour,* 1852, No. 5.

† Horne's Introduction, vol. i., pp. 13, 14.

and others,* but carried about with them the means of
destruction, of which they made use rather than fall into
the hands of their adversaries, as did Demosthenes,
Cato, Brutus, Cassius, and others. *Truth* was of small
account among many, even the best of heathens; for
they taught that, on many occasions, "*a* LIE *was to be
preferred to the* TRUTH *itself!*" In support of this startling statement, Mr. Horne quotes many passages from
Pagan writers.

One more statement with respect to the *moral and
social condition* of mankind under the Pagan system, and
my case is closed.

Slavery, the practice of buying, selling, and holding
in bondage human beings, was universal throughout the
Pagan world.

You will meet me with an objection, possibly, upon
this head, by reminding me that slavery was permitted
by the Almighty under the Jewish dispensation. It is
perfectly true that a modified bond-service was permitted
under the Mosaic economy, but the institution differed
most essentially from that which prevailed in Pagan
nations.

Slavery among the Jews could arise, legally, either
from captivity in war, insolvency, or from inability to
make restitution in case of theft. In the first case, it is
very doubtful whether modified bondage was not a merciful practice in the age in which Moses lived. The
horrible mutilations and other cruelties practised on
captives were so universal among the Gentile nations,
that bondage among the Jews would be a preferable
state of existence. In the other cases referred to, slavery

---

* Seneca, De Ira, lib. iii. c. 15.

was permitted by way of punishment, just as fraudulent insolvency and theft are punished among ourselves by deprivation of liberty.

Man-stealing, that is, taking an individual by force (except in the cases above alluded to), and selling him into slavery, or retaining him as a slave, is severely reprimanded by the law of Moses, *and made punishable with death.**

And with respect to the condition of those who could legally be detained in bondage under the Jewish law, the following most important modifications of the institution mark the position of the bond-servant as infinitely superior to that of the slave who groaned under the iron bondage of Pagan taskmasters.

They were to be treated with humanity (Lev. xxv. 39—55), and the injunction is enforced by the powerful argument, " For unto *Me*," says God, "*the children of Israel are servants*, they are *My servants*, whom I brought forth out of the land of Egypt." They were not to be punished severely; and, in case of the death of a servant, the master was amenable to punishment (Exodus xxi. 20, 21). If a master injured a bond-servant in eye, tooth, or member, he was to receive his freedom (Exodus xxi. 26, 27). They were to enjoy rest and religious privileges on every Sabbath-day and festival, so that, at least, one-seventh of their time was redeemed from labour (Exodus xx. 10; Deut. v. 14). They were to be invited to certain feasts (Deut. xii. 17, 18, etc.) They were to receive adequate subsistence (Deut. xxv. 4, etc.) The master was bound to provide for the marriage of a female servant, to take her to himself, or betroth her to his son (Exodus xxi. 8, *et seq.*) No servant of Hebrew

* Exod. xxi. 16; Deut. xxiv. 7.

origin could be obliged to serve more than six years, after which time he must be dismissed with his wife, and presents of considerable value (Exodus xxi. 2—4; Lev. xxv. 1—17). Even before the expiration of the six years, they might redeem themselves, or be redeemed by another, by purchase adequate in amount to the remaining years of service (Lev. xxv. 47—55). On the year of Jubilee, at the sounding of the silver trumpets, all Hebrew servants or slaves were to be emancipated (Lev. xxv. 40, 41). Slaves of Hebrew birth were permitted to hold property, as may be learned from Lev. xxv. 49, and 2 Sam. ix. 10; and, lastly, a fugitive slave from another nation, who sought refuge among the Hebrews, was to be received and treated kindly, *and not to be forcibly sent back again* (Deut. xxiii. 15, 16).

We see, then, that slavery, as it existed among the Jews, was, to those of Hebrew descent, little more than servitude or apprenticeship among ourselves; while the foreigner, taken captive in war, received better treatment than he could have expected in such times, had he fallen into the hands of Pagan idolaters; with the privilege of admission to the benefits of union with God's people, by right of circumcision, which was to be administered to him, and the enjoyment of a Sabbath of rest, and kind treatment, enjoined and enforced by the laws which regulated his master's conduct.

Nor must it be overlooked that the Mosaic economy was both *temporary and imperfect* (Heb. vii., viii., and xi., *passim*); and as our Lord explained that divorce was permitted by Moses on account of hardness of heart, so a modified bond-service was doubtless permitted on account of covetousness, which, in such times, would have resulted in gross cruelty and great destruction of life, unless it had been permitted a more convenient and merciful exercise in the retention of the services of captives.

Concerning slavery, as practised by professing Christians, a few words will be necessary in the next lecture.

And now I proceed, very briefly, to depict the condition of slaves under Pagan masters, particularly in Greece and Rome.

The practice appears to have been universally permitted and approved; not one philosopher has been found to object to it in its grossest forms : many of the more celebrated philosophers are known to have kept slaves themselves. Even Plato, in his " Perfect State," desires only that Greeks should not be enslaved. In Attica, a district not larger than an English county, there were at one time 150,000 slaves; while history informs us that at Rome, one Scaurus had 8000 slaves; and a Roman senator in the reign of Augustus, dying, left, with other property, 4116 slaves. In the reign of Julius Cæsar, the slaves were more numerous than the freemen, and the proportion afterwards assumed so alarming an aspect, both in Greece and Rome, that slaves were forbidden to wear a distinguishing dress, lest it should acquaint them with the fact of their numerical superiority. By the laws of Rome they were considered " chattels ;" were bought, sold, exchanged, without restraint; could be punished at the pleasure of their master, and put to death by him at his own will. They possessed *no legal rights*, any more than a horse or a cow may be said to have legal rights, and whatever treatment they received, could not appeal to any court of law, unless some humane citizen allowed the appeal to be made in his name. The property of the slave was the property of his master. I cannot say that the wife of the slave was his master's property also, for the Roman law considered the slave incapable of legal marriage, and therefore he had no wife; his children belonged to his master, and were sold or exchanged, as it pleased him. If examined at law, his testimony must be extorted by torture.

It is true that laws were made to restrain cruelty to slaves, and to ensure to them adequate sustenance; but as the slave had no right of appeal to the law, of what use could the law be to him? Some of these laws show the abject condition to which he was reduced: one law obliges masters to give each slave one pound of corn daily; another restrains mutilation of their persons, their limbs, and tongues; another prohibits the compulsion of slaves to combat with wild beasts at the shows, and requires for that purpose the license of the judicial authorities; another law forbids the forcible subjection of female slaves to prostitution; while it transpires that one Pollio, a knight in the time of Augustus, and a friend of that emperor, was "reprobated" for his irregular conduct, in throwing slaves alive into a pond to feed lampreys for his table.* It was a practice with men of rank to keep slaves in a state of nudity, chained up at the doors of their dwellings—your equals and mine, in the sight of God, possessed of mental powers and immortal souls—converted into watch-dogs. The story of Lazarus, which you read in the New Testament, is no exaggerated picture, when applied to Rome at *the height of her civilization.* "Moreover, the dogs came and licked

* Art. *Pollio Vedius,* Lempriere's "Classical Dictionary."

his sores." Dogs, more merciful than man, when his mind is altogether alienated from God. This is no libel. The office of the chained, wounded, and hopeless creatures was to warn the household in case of attempted assassination (a daily occurrence at that period). As gratitude could not, of course, be expected to influence the slave, fear was resorted to as a motive; it was death to the watch-dog if the master fell. The slave had the option of death by the assassin, if faithful, or death by his master, if silent; and history mentions, incidentally, two such cases, in one of which two slaves suffered, and in the other, the *four hundred* slaves of Pedanius Secundus were put to death.*

> " Slaves to be lash'd and tortur'd and resold,
> Or maim'd or murder'd for a fine of gold.
> Helots degraded, scarce esteem'd as man,
> Having no rights, for ever under ban,
> *Were half the world* when ancient Homer sung,
> And wit and wisdom flowed from Plato's tongue.
> Slaves were the swarming multitudes of Rome,
> Having no hope, no thought of better doom ;—
> Fetter'd in body and enslaved in mind,
> Their mental eyeballs sear, and dark, and blind,
> They crawl'd mere brutes, and if they dar'd complain,
> *Were lash'd and tortur'd until tame again !" †

But I must gather up my subject to bring it to a conclusion.

I have set before you the leading features of Paganism,

---

* Tacitus, Annal. xiv. pp. 42—44. The principal facts regarding slavery have been gathered from Jahn's "Archæologia Biblica," the Cyclopædia of the Society for Diffusing Useful Knowledge, and Maunder's "Scientific and Literary Treasury," article *Slavery.* Also Horne's Introduction, vol. i. pp. 12, 13.

† Dr. Mackay's " Hope of the World."

the system which swayed the world in the Augustan age. I have told you somewhat of the character of that system; its pantheistic, sacerdotal, and ceremonial nature. I have hinted at the gross obscenity and spoken of the flagrant cruelty of its rites. I have endeavoured to convey a just idea of the moral and social condition of the world under its influence ; its effects upon the morality and the happiness of children, females, rulers, people, and slaves.

The picture is indeed a dark, a revolting one ; any one who attentively and thoughtfully reads the history of those times, must become convinced that mankind, with few exceptions, had become as degraded, as sinful, as ignorant of truth, as cruel, as vindictive, and withal as *wretched*, as it is possible to conceive. Revenge, public and private, had come to be accounted virtue. War, bloodshed, and violence conferred the highest glory ; shame and decency, both public and private, were well-nigh lost ; the cruelty and ferocity of the people were such, that the blood shed for their gratification would have more than satiated a community of tigers.

Things which in our days would create a riot if *attempted*, then created riots when *prevented ;* while man had universally enslaved his fellow-man. With all this the greatest insecurity of life existed ; all went armed everywhere, a needful precaution, for assassinations and poisonings were of daily occurrence, and men were not ashamed to ask of the gods to speed the dagger or the poison bowl. Thinking men were longing, hoping, and looking, they knew not to whom, for deliverance, being filled with terror or with loathing at what they witnessed. Every Pagan god they could invent, or borrow from conquered nations, had his altars and his temples, and was supplicated for relief; from "the likeness of corruptible man and birds and four-footed beasts," they descended to deify the very *sinks and sewers, diseases, passions, vermin, and vices,* until all hope of remedy appears to have been given up.

Plato's opinion has been already quoted—"men had sunk lower than the basest of the brutes." Pliny writes: "Nothing certain upon earth is to be found, and nothing is found so *miserable* yet so proud as *man.*" Tacitus anticipates the end of the world, "on account of the corruptions of *mankind.*" Seneca writes : "*All is replete with crime, and vice everywhere abounds. More evil is committed than can possibly be healed; the struggle and confusion are becoming more desperate, while lust daily grows into sin; shame is rapidly declining; veneration for what is pure and good is unknown; every one yields to his own lusts. Vice no longer hides in secret, it is made public to all eyes; depravity has so far advanced, that innocence has become not only more rare, but is now a thing* ALTOGETHER UNKNOWN."*

And what is the lesson which we learn from the subject of to-night's lecture ?

THAT NEITHER LEARNING, NOR CIVILIZATION, NOR PHILOSOPHY, NOR ALL OF THEM COMBINED, CAN OF THEMSELVES MAKE PEOPLE EITHER VIRTUOUS OR HAPPY.

Contrasted with our own times and country a marked difference is observable, both as it regards morality and the social condition of all classes : there is now more of security, of virtue, of solid comfort and happiness in society, in families and with individuals. I am not prepared to-night, even if time permitted, to enter into the

* Seneca, De Ira, ii. cap. 8.

question, "to what is this difference to be attributed?" but I will simply observe that, whatever it may be, it is *not* civilization, *not* the cultivation of arts and of letters, *not* the study of philosophy ; for, observe, all these had arrived at the greatest perfection in the ancient world, when the greatest depravity and wretchedness prevailed. The Augustan age has become proverbial, as I stated in the outset, for the encouragement given to the fine arts, to literature, and to learning. We have no sculptors whose works can compare with those of Phidias and Praxiteles ; no architecture which can exceed in excellence the Parthenon at Athens, or the Forum at Rome ; no epic poet like Virgil; no lyrical poet to excel Horace ; of original and profound thinkers we have none like Plato and Seneca ; no historians more gifted than the Plinys, than Tacitus, than Sallust, than Plutarch ; no actor like Roscius, nor orator to excel Cicero.

Our ameliorated condition, then, must be attributable to some other influence than that of mere learning, or civilization, or cultivation of the arts ; and the lesson, so far as we can learn it to-night, appears to be that *the "world by* wisdom *(philosophy) knew not God."* *

The remarks of a recent writer,† applying to the great Assyrian empire, which had well-nigh passed away before Rome was founded, are so applicable to the case of Rome and of Grece, and to all the Pagan empires of antiquity, and are withal so suited for the consideration of ourselves, in these days, that I quote them as an appropriate conclusion and improvement to this lecture :—

---

* 1 Cor. i. 21.

† "Nineveh : its Rise and Ruin." By Rev. J. Blackburn, p. 142, second edition.

"It is plain that human nature amongst the Assyrians was not, physically or intellectually, in an infantile or dwarfish state. If we contemplate their figures upon the sculptured panels in our Museum, we must acknowledge their frames were finely developed, and that they have the aspect of a brave and noble race, fitly compared by the prophet to lions, in their terrible presence and majestic bearing. And if we mark their intellectual progress, as seen in their discoveries in astronomy, their taste in art, their knowledge and skill in manufactures, their power and prowess in arms, we must confess that they betray no signs of intellectual feebleness. And yet, with all these advantages, what were they? Avaricious, lewd, drunken, lawless, oppressive, cruel. The scenes of re- finement, splendour, and magnificence which surrounded them gave, perhaps, grace and dignity to their man- ners, but no purity to their characters, nor kindness to their hearts. Like all the great nations of antiquity that surrounded or succeeded them, they were the victims of ignorance and vice, of war and despotism. The first object of all governments—the happiness of the people— was never considered by their rulers ; and consequently they were used as the tools of sanguinary princes and idolatrous priests, who placed national happiness and glory in martial spoils and constrained proselytes. The slavery they imposed upon their miserable captives must often have been more bitter than death. *It is, in fact, plain from all history, whether of nations or individuals, that the knowledge of arts and letters is not sufficient to renew the heart or life of those who cultivate them.* Emi- nent attainments in both have been made by men destitute of moral sense, and the slaves of every low, selfish, de- grading vice. They have lived amidst the loveliest scenes of nature and of art ; all the soft and elevating influences of the beautiful and the sublime have fallen upon them in vain ; and the fairest countries have witnessed the foulest crimes. Whilst, then, we rejoice in the progress of art, science, and literature amongst ourselves, and are thankful to witness museums and menageries, picture-galleries, and schools of art, parks, and pleasure-gardens, provided for the people—and admit that these occupations may divert their attention from grosser and more grovelling pursuits—yet we hold that all these are compatible with proud, selfish, sensual, and godless hearts, manifesting both misanthropy towards their fellow-men and a haughty rebellion against the Most High. IT IS BY THE INFLU-ENCE OF DIVINE TRUTH ALONE THAT MEN ARE TO BE RE-STORED TO A HAPPY CONFORMITY TO THE MORAL CHARACTER OF GOD.

LECTURE II.

CHRISTIANITY.

" To give light to them that sit in darkness and the shadow of death."—Luke i. 79.

Our last lecture closed amidst the gloom and shadows of Pagan darkness. We left man, who had shut his eyes to the light of natural religion—or that which may be learned of God from Nature—and with whom the last glimmering of primeval revelation had gone out, groping his way in almost utter hopelessness of finding any light to guide his forlorn footsteps. We listened to the complainings and forebodings of virtuous men ; we noted the reckless depravity of the bad. It is now my office to inform you that, amidst all that called for despondency and despair, there existed, nevertheless, a very prevalent anticipation of deliverance—an almost universal looking or waiting for a deliverer. It is true this idea was undefined, and consequently imperfectly appreciated, but it was generally entertained among all the nations whose literature has, to any extent, come down to us ; and, what is more worthy of remark, the expectation had reached its height at the Augustan age—the period to which I particularly refer in these lectures.

The Hindoos were expecting another *Avata*, or incarnation of their chief god, and that Avata a most important one as it regarded the destinies of the human race. Among the Persians, who followed the teaching of

Zoroaster, their *Sosiosh,* "Man of the World," was expected. The Chinese, according to Confucius, were " to
look for the holy one from the west." The Pythian oracle
among the Greeks and the Etruscan priests in Italy had
alike predicted their own overthrow. The Sybil prophetess
had spoken of the coming of the Lord of the earth.*
Chaldean astrologers travelled, as you know, to Judea,
prepared with kingly gifts to offer to the expected deliverer.† Herod, the governor of Judea, entertained the
same expectation, and consulted the council of the Sanhe-
drim as to the birth-place of this great One ; being informed that the Jewish prophet had foretold it should be
at Bethlehem, he sent and killed all the young children
there, hoping to compass his destruction. Devout Jews,
such as Simeon and Anna, were waiting in the Jewish
temple for his appearance, convinced that the time was
at hand.‡

So we see that ancient writers gave currency to the
tradition ; crafty Pagan priests and pretended prophets
worked up the popular belief into feigned communications
from heaven ; cruel rulers dreaded that which all anticipated ; and holy men and women waited for the " consolation of Israel" and of the world. All of them, good
and bad, are witnesses of a prevalent anticipation of
coming interference in the affairs of men.

But Rome is more especially the field of our inquiry ;
and as she has left to our times a large mass of literature,
we may expect to find there especial reference to this
looking for deliverance from evil. Suetonius, the Roman
historian, says : " An ancient and settled persuasion
prevailed, throughout the East, that the Fates had de-

* Mühleisen's " Genuine and Spurious Religion," vol. i. p. 185.
† Matt. ii. 1, 2.   ‡ Luke ii. 25—35, 36—38.

creed some one to proceed from Judea, who should attain *universal* empire.* Tacitus writes : " Many were persuaded that it was contained in the ancient books of their priests, that at that very time the East should prevail, and that some one should proceed from Judea, and possess the dominion."† Josephus and Philo both state that there existed the same expectation.

About the time when Augustus was born—some sixty years B.C.—the anticipated coming of a king, a conqueror, or a deliverer had even passed into a proverb—was referred to in the senate, and was the theme of the poets.

Virgil wrote a Pastoral complimenting the Roman consul Pollio on the birth of a son, whom, in the spirit of flattery, he describes as the predicted deliverer. The substance of the Pastoral is said to have been borrowed from a prophecy delivered by the Sybil. The following lines form part of a translation of the ode :—

> " The last great age, foretold by sacred rhymes,
> Renews its finished course : Saturnian times
> Roll round again ; and mighty years, begun
> From their first orb, in radiant circles run.
> The base, degen'rate, iron offspring ends ;
> A golden progeny from heaven descends.
> The father banish'd virtue shall restore ;
> And crimes shall threat the guilty world no more.
> The son shall lead the life of gods, and be
> By gods and heroes seen, and gods and heroes see.
> The jarring nations he in peace shall bind,
> And with paternal virtues rule mankind." ‡

As another indication of this prevalent expectation,

---

* Suet., Vespasian, cap. 4.   † Tacitus, Annals, v. 13.
‡ Virgil, fourth Pastoral.

the Emperor Augustus, born about this time, having his nativity cast by Nigidius Figulus, an astrologer and mathematician, it was predicted of him that he should be Lord of the earth; he was deified during his lifetime by his flatterers, temples were erected to him, and his worship established; his name, originally Octavianus, was altered to *Augustus*, sacred, and in the Greek, to *Sebastos*, adorable. Our eighth month still bears his name.

Such were the prevailing longings of good men, the fears of bad men, and pride of ambitious men, respecting the advent of a king and deliverer. These anticipations explain, at the same time that they confirm, the prophecies of Scripture delivered long before the event, particularly the prophecy of Haggai, 520 years before Christ: "For thus saith the Lord of Hosts : Yet once, it is a little while, and I will shake the heavens, and the earth, and the sea, and the dry land ; and I will shake (agitate) all nations, and *the desire of all nations* shall come."*

In the physical world, it has often been noticed that the most intense darkness precedes the first dawning of the day: in the course of the world's history, it has frequently happened that the period of the greatest discord and confusion has been but the harbinger of prosperity and peace. It was so with the era to which our lectures refer: the uncertainty and perplexity of mind, the darkness of the moral atmosphere, and the violence of the storms of human passions, were about to usher in the dawnings of light, purity, and peace.

It is now about 1877—8 years ago (a few months more

* Haggai ii. 6, 7.

or less),* but certainly in the reign of Augustus Cæsar,
that a most remarkable person appeared in this our world,
and wrought an extraordinary innovation upon existing
systems. By birth and station he ranked as an artizan—
one of your own class, so the Evangelists inform us;
tradition has added, perhaps correctly, that he pursued,
with his reputed father, the trade of a carpenter; and our
English version of the Bible has endorsed the tradition.

The world, as I have told you, was then intently
awaiting the coming of some great one; but it was certainly not looking for his advent in the lower ranks of
life. The appearance I allude to attracted, therefore,
little attention. His birth was, however, remarkably
attested by prodigies, such as the appearance of an unusual star, and visions of angels. It happened at the
period pointed out by Daniel;† at the place indicated by
Micah;‡ at the time of a census of the inhabitants of
Judea, taken by Augustus, the Roman emperor. This
registration disclosed officially the fact that, both by the
mother's and the reputed father's side, he was of the
lineage of the royal house of David, of the tribe of
Judah, of the family of Abraham: all of which had been
distinctly predicted in the Jewish Scriptures.

It is not my intention to detail the remarkable facts
connected with His birth, life and death; many of you
are fully acquainted with them, and all of you have the

---

* Jesus Christ was born from about four to six years before
the commencement of the common Christian era—at what period
of the year is not known. The error in the computation of
the period occurred about A.D. 527. *Vide* Archbishop Usher's
" Chronology," also Dr. Kitto's " Daily Bible Illustrations," Life
and Death of our Lord, 29th week, 6th day, under Matt. ii. 1.

† Daniel ix. 25—27.   ‡ Micah v. 2.

fullest facilities for informing yourselves concerning them. He claimed to be no less than the Son of God; to be one with God; in short, "the desire of all nations," the Messiah, the expected deliverer of Jews and Gentiles. It forms no part of my purpose to enter upon the argument as to the truthfulness of these claims. Some of you admit them, with all their consequences, and possibly some of you do not, or may not have fully investigated the foundations upon which they rest. You will all of you feel that it is a question too important to hurry over or to treat slightly; nor could the evidences be brought fully before you in the course of a single lecture. At other times, in other places, I affectionately advise you, if you have not done so already, to study the subject with humble and teachable minds. The investigation of such a subject is surely not unworthy of any one of you, nor, indeed, of the highest human intelligence; for some of the loftiest intellects which have conferred lustre on our species have undertaken the study, and submitted unreservedly to His claims.

It is rather with the *historical facts*, and the *doctrine* which Christ introduced, that we have to do; and with these, of necessity, treated very briefly.

He asserted, then, that His mission was undertaken to heal and to save a sin-stricken world; that He might be a light to those who sat in darkness, and lead all those who would follow His guidance to peace, to holiness, and to heaven. He lived, so far as the facts of His life have been communicated, only to do good to the bodies and souls of men, and to propagate, inculcate, and explain His doctrines. He associated with the humble, the illiterate, the needy, and the sinful. He refused kingly honours when offered to Him, and discountenanced all ideas of worldly rule or aggrandizement, as unsuited to His kingdom, which He explained to be spiritual in its nature. He died (contrary to the expectation of all His followers) as a malefactor, by the hands of the Roman government, at the instigation of His disappointed countrymen, the Jews—as He, and the prophets before Him, had oftentimes predicted. At His death, as at His birth, prodigies occurred, such as an earthquake, and a supernatural darkness at a period when no eclipse of the sun, according to the laws of Nature, could possibly happen;* which prodigies were reported to the authorities at Rome.†

And, to render his story the most remarkable in the world's history (irrespective of its importance in a religious aspect), He forsook the grave, as predicted, in

---

* All eclipses of the sun must happen at the time of *new* moon. Jesus Christ was crucified at the Feast of the Passover, always celebrated at the *full* moon.

† That the prodigies which attended the Crucifixion did *not* pass without notice at Rome is certain, notwithstanding the statement to the contrary made by Gibbon, in his "Decline and Fall of the Roman Empire" (vol. ii. p. 379). That false statement has been dealt with at length, and annihilated by Mr. Hartwell Horne, in his "Introduction to the Critical Study and Knowledge of the Scriptures" (Unabridged Edition, vol. i., chap. iii. p. 187). It may be useful, however, to cite here the two authorities which are most conclusive upon this point. The darkness and earthquake are both expressly referred to by Celsus, the bitter and acute adversary of Christianity, as *facts* which he was unable to deny ("Origen contra Celsum," lib. ii. 55, p. 94); and Tertullian, in addressing his Pagan adversaries, asserts, without fear of contradiction, "at the moment of Christ's death, the light departed from the sun, and the land was darkened at noonday; *which wonder is related in* YOUR OWN ANNALS, *and is preserved in* YOUR ARCHIVES TO THIS DAY" (Tertullian, "Apol.," c. 21).

spite of a Roman guard, and appeared to His friends and followers repeatedly during forty days, and then disappeared from their sight.

The reality of these facts has been testified as no other events of history were ever confirmed. In no less than five separate histories were they recorded by those who were eye-witnesses; while many other books, written by parties to the transactions, refer to and confirm their truth. And what is even more remarkable, the witnesses of these facts travelled over land and sea to spread the intelligence, without any of the usual motives which influence men, and with no personal interests to serve; *who gained nothing by their assertions but persecution, scorn, and contempt; and who, the greater part of them, laid down their lives gladly as witnesses to the truth of their statements.*

I repeat that no single fact of history has been so abundantly verified as the facts connected with the life and death and resurrection of Christ; and he that rejects these truths must be prepared to credit—firstly, that at least some one hundred and twenty individuals entered into a conspiracy to propagate a falsehood, with nothing to gain by it, but, on the contrary, prepared to undergo loss of all the world values, even life itself; secondly, that such parties, although guilty of falsehood, inculcated and practised virtue, unusual and extraordinary for such, or indeed for any times; thirdly, that all of them persisted in the assertion of a falsehood until death, without disclosing the nature of the conspiracy which existed, or the deceptions they had practised; and, fourthly, that many of them sealed their witness with their blood, when confession of their error, had it been such, would have saved their lives.

Who is the credulous man, think you? He who accepts a statement supported by all the eye-witnesses, and uncontradicted by those who would have contradicted if they could; or the man who disbelieves every one, but believes in all the extraordinary consequences which I have shown must result from falsehood, had it existed?

I must now leave *the facts* relating to the introduction of Christianity, and consider, also very briefly, the nature of the *doctrine*, or teaching, introduced by Christ; in other words, the *character of the system termed* CHRISTIANITY. This, it will be observed, admits of no argument as to its reality. Although much misunderstood, and, it may be, misrepresented, Christianity is a fact of which no one has been bold enough to deny the existence.

And first I would remark, that Christianity constituted a wondrous *innovation* upon the views of the world, both Jewish and Pagan. It was no adaptation, no mere reformation; no compromise was entered into. The language of Christ, on more than one occasion, was to the effect, "Behold, I make all things new." He explained to his astonished followers, by figures, that as new wine could not conveniently be put into perishing skins, and as it would be inappropriate to patch up, with new cloth, worn-out garments, so His system was to supersede and set aside those systems which were decayed, had "waxed old," and were "ready to vanish away." The religion of Christianity, in short, effected a *revolution*, and cannot be viewed in the light either of a *restoration*, a *reformation*, or a *reconstruction*.

It formed an *entire contrast* to existing Paganism; an

outline of the leading features of the two systems will convey to your minds a clear perception of their strong antagonism.

Paganism was, as already explained, *polytheistic;* Christ taught that God was *one.*

Paganism represented God in the likeness of *visible objects,* such as "corruptible men and birds, and four-footed beasts, and creeping things." Christianity represented Him as a *Spirit,* "whom no man hath seen or can see;" "eternal, immortal, invisible."

Paganism was in its services *formal, external, ceremonial, and local.* Christ taught that henceforth religion would be acceptable only as it was *spiritual and of the heart.* "They that worship must worship Him in spirit and in truth;" "for the Father seeketh such to worship Him."

Paganism was essentially *sacerdotal.* Christianity teaches that a *mediatorial and sacrificial priesthood* is no longer needed; that Christ had opened "a new and living way" of access to God, and invited all His followers to come unto God directly "*through Him.*"

Paganism, like Judaism, appointed *continually recurring sacrifices* for transgression. Christianity teaches that "Christ was *once offered* to bear the sins of many," and "by *one offering* He had *perfected for ever* them that are sanctified."

For cruel, costly, and cumbersome *rites and offerings,* Christ substituted *faith,* with *love to God and love to man.*

In lieu of *purchased* pardon, attainable among Pagans by means of costly offerings, Christ offered salvation and pardon *freely* to the poorest, "without money and without price." While Paganism initiated only *the wealthy, the wise, or the worthy* to its mysteries, Christ ordered His message to be carried especially to the *poor, to the sinful, and the simple,* and Himself set the example.

So far from sanctioning *immorality* or *sensuality,* which Paganism encouraged and promoted, Christ taught that even the *thoughts of the heart* should be watched and controlled, and that the guilty emotion indulged was equivalent to sin in action; and He pronounced His blessing, and the promise of a sight of God's presence, to the *"pure in heart."*

So far from sanctioning *cruelty,* Christ taught, "Blessed are the merciful, for they shall obtain mercy."

So far from honouring *revenge* or *hatred,* so universal with Pagans, Christ taught the, till then unheard of, doctrine, "I say unto you, *love your enemies;* do good to them which hate you; and pray for them that despitefully use you and persecute you." He led the way in this difficult path by praying for His murderers, "Father, forgive them, for they know not what they do."

So far from justifying *murder* by way of retaliation, accounted meritorious among Pagans, Christ taught that to be angry, without just cause, with a brother, the irritating word, and the unkind judgment, *all were classed by Him with the deprivation of life.*

To sum up: war, aggressive or revengeful, bloodshedding, rapine, oppression, slavery—almost the entire practices of Paganism—Christ unequivocally condemned. He cut up by the root all excuse for such practices, by the commands, "Thou shalt love thy neighbour as thyself;" "whatsoever ye would that men should do unto you, do ye even so to them;" and when one asked Him for the definition of the term, " *neighbour,*" He answered by a parable, " *Your bitterest foe.*" *

I have given you necessarily a very brief and imperfect sketch of the facts connected with the founding of Christianity, and the character of the system so called. And here I would say to you, as *working men,* do not consider it any indignity, but rather an honour, to be termed by that name ; labour is honourable, more honourable than idleness, even though it be dignified by titles and gilded by wealth. God has shown respect for honest labour, by creating man fitted for it, and by making him miserable without it; by appointing our common progenitor to " dress and to keep" the garden in which he was placed; and, above all, by *permitting His Son to pass the greater part of His life on earth,* in the workshop of a Jewish artificer.

> " Sixty centuries have failed to teach
> The dignity, the beauty, and the joy,
> The piety and usefulness of work !
> 'Tis but *excess* of labour that is pain—
> Just as excess of food, or wine, or rest,
> Or any blessing that mankind abuse."

Never believe any who shall tell you that God inflicted the *curse of labour* on man ; his organization, muscular and nervous, contradicts it; your own experience denies it, and, above all, the Word of God repudiates the statement. The *ground* has been cursed for man's rebellion, and his labour, as you well know, is often *excessive* and ill-requited, but there is more of mercy than of judgment in that labour still.

But to proceed: Christianity, born in Judea, very soon reached Rome, the world's metropolis. The exact time of its arrival there is unknown, but it is not im-

* Vile Sermon on the Mount, and New Testament, *passim.*

probable that it was carried there by some of those three thousand Christians,* the fruits of Peter's address on the day of Pentecost, when he exercised the high privilege conferred upon him of unlocking "the kingdom of heaven" by the preaching of Christ crucified to that crowd of converts from "every nation under heaven."† We are distinctly informed that there were amongst his hearers "*strangers of Rome—Jews and proselytes*," that is, Jews from Rome, native born, and proselytes from among the Romans to Judaism; and if any of these were converted, they would immediately carry Christianity to Rome on their return thither. Be this as it may, it is quite clear that there were Christians at Rome in the reign of Claudius, or about A.D. 52, say within twenty-five years of the death of Christ. For Suetonius, a Pagan writer at Rome, says the Jews raised tumults at Rome at the instigation of Chrestus (Christ, of whose death he, as a Pagan, was ignorant), and were banished accordingly by the Emperor Claudius.‡ This Pagan testimony agrees exactly with the statement made by Luke,§ that Paul, the apostle, found at Corinth, in Greece, "a certain Jew named Aquila, lately come from Italy with his wife Priscilla; because that *Claudius had commanded all Jews to depart from Rome.*" That Aquila and Priscilla were *Christianized* Jews, previously to their departure from Rome, there can be little doubt, for their conversion at Corinth is not mentioned; they associated with Paul in their daily labour as tent-makers; were the means of instructing Apollos in the "way of God more

---

* Acts ii. 41. † Acts ii. 5.

‡ Suetonius, Claud., c. 25 : " Judæos, impulsore Chresto assidue tumultuantes, Româ expulit."

§ Acts xviii. 1, 2.

perfectly;" assisted Paul in his apostolic labours, and had a church in their house.*

Christianity, then, and persecution on account of it, had both found place at Rome in the reign of Claudius within twenty-five years from the death of its founder. Some five or six years later, about 57 to 59 A.D., the Apostle Paul wrote a letter to the Christians at Rome, called by us the " Epistle to the Romans." In this letter he speaks of his strong desire to visit them, and thanks God that their "faith is spoken of throughout the whole world;"† and in the concluding portions of the letter, sends his Christian salutations to so many persons and households, that it is quite clear that Christianity had not been then very recently established, and, moreover, that it had made some progress at that time in Rome.

It may not be very *important* to ascertain the exact period when the religion of Christ began to be known at Rome, but it will, I think, be *interesting* to show its early introduction there, and the opposition it created in the reign of Claudius, when we come to consider the local position of the Catacombs, to which I must presently refer, and couple all the facts with the circumstances related concerning the first arrival of the Apostle Paul at the Imperial city.

About two years later than the date of his letter, Paul visited Rome, as related in the Acts of the Apostles, as a prisoner under course of trial, he having appealed to Nero the then Roman emperor. If you will refer to the map of the Mediterranean Sea, you will notice the course which the Apostle took in his voyage to Rome, as recorded in the last chapter of the Acts of the Apostles; from Melita or Malta, where he suffered shipwreck, to Syracuse

* Compare Acts xviii. 2, 3, 26; Rom. xvi. 3—5; and 1 Cor. xvi. 19.   † Rom. i. 8, 10, 11.

on the coast of Sicily, where he tarried three days; thence to Rhegium, the southern point of Italy; thence to Puteoli, and so onwards to Appii Forum, "the marketplace of Appius," about fifty-six miles, and to the "Three Taverns," about thirty miles from Rome. These two places were situated on the Appian Way, a road leading south from Rome. You will notice that Christian brethren came to meet him even "as far as Appii Forum," that is, fifty-six miles on the road,* a circumstance remarkably indicating the affection of these early Christians for the Apostle. Now it was under and along the line of this Appian Way, which Paul traversed in his journey to Rome, that the Catacombs—the hiding-places of the early Christians—had been excavated.

Looking to the fact of the opposition to Christianity manifested in the reign of Claudius, the circumstance stated by Paul, that *no man stood by him, but that all forsook him* at his first examination before Nero,† and the admission of the Jews at that very place and period, "for as concerning this sect, we know that *everywhere it is spoken against*,"‡ I think I may assume that even at that early period the Christians, influenced by a regard for their safety, had commenced taking refuge from popular dislike, Jewish opposition, and the persecution of the Roman Government, in these subterranean fastnesses, which have been found to extend at least *fifteen miles from Rome in the direction of the Appian Way.* This is, at all events, an interesting speculation, and may account for these poor people being able to meet Paul at so great a distance from Rome.

We are not, however, left long to conjecture as to the state of things as it regarded Christianity at Rome. The

* Acts xxviii. 15. † 2 Tim. iv. 16. ‡ Acts xxviii. 22.

storm of persecution, so repeatedly predicted by their Lord and Master, was about to break upon His followers, and before the close of the sanguinary reign of the monster Nero, they were doubtless glad to take refuge in these "dens and caves of the earth."

It is not my intention, in these lectures, to follow the history of the Christian Church at Rome in its early struggles, and to narrate the persecutions which it experienced; it will be sufficient for me to state, that the first well-authenticated instance of persecution occurred under Nero, about the year A.D. 64, soon after Paul's first visit. Tacitus narrates the circumstances very fully, and, being a Pagan, regards the Christian sect from that point of view. In the tenth year of Nero the city was nearly destroyed by fire, which continued burning eight days, and out of fourteen divisions only eight remained entire. So great was the indignation of the populace, who charged Nero with having intentionally caused the fire, that he found bribes to men and offerings to the gods alike useless, and with the view of appeasing the people, he attributed the crime to the despised Christians. These are the words of Tacitus :—

"The infamy of that horrible transaction still adhered to him. To suppress, if possible, this common rumour, Nero procured others to be accused and punished with exquisite tortures : a race of men detested for their evil (?) practices, who were commonly known by the name of Christians. The author of this sect was Christus, who in the reign of Tiberius was punished with death as a criminal by the procurator Pontius Pilate. At first those only were apprehended who confessed themselves of this sect, afterwards a *vast multitude* discovered by them ; all of whom were condemned, not so much for the crime of burning the city as for their enmity to mankind. Their executions were so contrived as to expose them to derision and contempt. Some were covered over with the skins of wild beasts, that they might be torn to pieces by dogs ; some were crucified ; while others, having been *daubed over with combustible materials, were set up as lights in the night-time and thus burned to death.* For these spectacles Nero gave his own gardens, and at the same time exhibited there the diversions of the circus, until at length these men, though really criminal and deserving exemplary punishment, began to be commiserated as people who were destroyed, not out of regard to the public welfare, but only to gratify the cruelty of one man."*

At his second visit to Rome, Paul was put to death by Nero. From this date onwards, history identifies the Christians at Rome with the Catacombs there. The persecutions were repeated again and again, under different emperors, during several centuries, and many of the edicts authorizing the persecutions commence with a prohibition to enter and take refuge in these hiding-places —the rescript of Valerian and Gallienus, for instance ; at the close of a persecution, Gallienus gave the Christians a formal licence to return to the Catacombs.†

But it is time for me to introduce you to this cradle of Christianity at Rome; to take you by the hand and lead you through its tortuous windings, explaining what appears mysterious, directing your attention to that which is interesting, gathering instruction as we proceed, and closing with such moral improvement as the circumstances are calculated to afford.

* Tacitus, Annal. xv. c. 44.
† Maitland's "Church in the Catacombs," p. 38 ; Eusebius, Hist. Eccles. ib. vii. c. 13.

The word *catacomb* means literally a subterranean excavation, but has been applied in recent times to excavated places of burial; the extensive quarries in the vicinity of many large cities having been used for such purposes. Thus, at Syracuse, Alexandria, Naples, and Paris, as well as at Rome, there exist extensive excavations used as receptacles for the dead. Those at Rome, however, exceed all others in extent, and surpass them in interest.

In the latter days of the Republic, and during the reigns of the first Cæsars, the city of Rome increased exceedingly in extent and magnificence. It was the boast of Augustus that "he had found Rome brick, and had left it marble." To procure the material necessary for these public works the soil around the city was quarried in many directions. The material obtained was a soft, sandy stone, of volcanic origin, termed *tufa* and *puzzolana*.

There were other excavations in Rome—those of the Esquiline Hill, outside the gate of that name; from these pits sand was obtained, used for making cement, as recommended by Vitruvius, the architect, as preferable to all others for that purpose.* These sandpits of the Esquiline Hill must not be confounded with the excavations, chiefly south of Rome, called the Christian Catacombs, as it is clear that the former were never used as Christian cemeteries, but were receptacles for the bodies of Pagans. At the period to which I refer, it was the custom for the Pagan Romans to burn their dead, and to preserve only the ashes. Those, however, who perished by the hand of the law, by lightning, and also suicides, were forbidden the usual rites of burial : while the lower orders of the people, and slaves, could not afford the honours of a

* Maitland, pp. 24, 25.

/

80

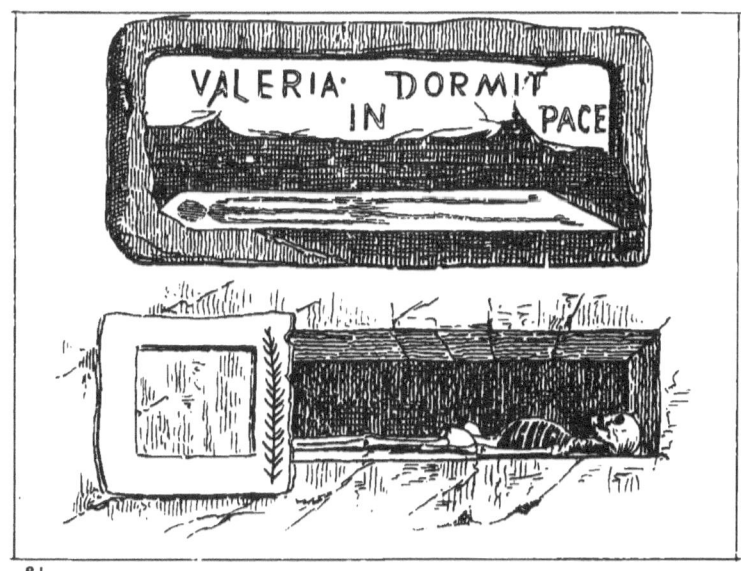

81

TOMBS & INSCRIBED SLABS.

funeral pile. Their bodies were therefore cast without ceremony down these pits, where they putrefied, much to the annoyance of the inhabitants of Rome ; and the pits were termed, accordingly, *puticulæ*, from the Latin word, which signifies to putrefy. These Esquiline pits were evidently closed in the reign of Augustus,* before the introduction of Christianity to the world, and therefore they contain only the bodies of Pagans, and will not be referred to again in these lectures.

I return now to the consideration of the Catacombs— the excavated galleries which were used, as hiding or burial-places, exclusively by the Christians, as appears by the inscriptions, and by the fact of the dead having been buried there entire in separate graves, and neither reduced to ashes nor heaped together in pits, like the bodies of Pagans.

We will set out on our journey along one of the high roads which lead out of Rome, the Via Flaminia, the Via Ostiensis, or perhaps, better than all, the Via Appia, and visit the extensive Catacombs named after St. Sebastian, which lie in that quarter. We enter through a low, dark doorway, upon an aisle, which divides into branches running in various directions,—all losing themselves in the darkness which envelops objects at the distance of a few feet ; but we will light our candles and torches, and proceed cautiously, attended by a guide who knows something of the intricate windings of the labyrinth. [80.] The galleries are about eight or ten feet high, and from four to six feet in width. Tombs, rifled of their contents or from which the slabs which closed them have been removed, yawn around you, tier above tier in never-ending succes-

* Horace, Satires, i. 8.

sion : here is one larger than others—it is a *bisomum*, or grave for two ; here a passage branches off to the left—it is unsafe to traverse, for the puzzolana has fallen in blocks ; on the right, another has been walled up with masonry, as a measure of precaution, as strangers have strayed, lost their way, and never been heard of. We arrive at a part of the gallery so obstructed with rubbish, that we must crawl on hands and knees, if we would further explore in this direction. But here are rough and dangerous stairs descending; they lead to a lower labyrinth of galleries and crypts, and if we explore these, we shall find a third and sometimes a fourth range of excavations, one below the other. Here is a wider space, at the junction of four branching galleries, it is slightly domed at the summit ; and there is a chain which once suspended a lamp ; and there are tombs arranged with more regard to order, and inscriptions which speak of holy men and women, and rude sculptures and primitive paintings of Scripture subjects. It is a place of gathering, where the early Christians met to worship their God and Saviour. But what is it makes the air fresher, the breathing more easy here ? the atmosphere does not taste so hot and dusty and earthy. Look, there is an air-hole and a glimmer of daylight from above ; it is one of the *luminaria cryptæ* or shafts, which lighted and ventilated these subterranean abodes, and which are still found at intervals perforating the soil about the Campagna, near Rome, indicating the extent and direction of the ramifying galleries beneath.

You will be glad now to ascend to the upper air while I tell you something of the *extent* of these Catacombs. Some of the cemeteries contain galleries which extend probably two or three miles, with branches in all directions, and no one now living is personally acquainted with more than a small portion of them. A German traveller of the last century says, that to visit all parts of the Catacombs of St. Sebastian, would be to undertake *a walk of twenty miles*, and that he thought, that if the length of all the passages, crypts, and galleries could be summed up and put together, there might be *one hundred miles* of this subterranean Rome; but, in his time, many of the galleries were walled up, several bewildered persons having perished in them.* It is clear that all the Catacombs have not as yet been discovered and explored; for during the French occupation of Rome, further discoveries have been made and are still making, and very large collections of drawings and of works of art have been recently brought to Paris by M. Perret, an enterprising French architect.†

And now as to the *occupation and contents of the Catacombs.* They were used, as I have before stated, as places of refuge from the storm of persecution, which, commencing at or about the time of Nero, beat upon the first followers of Christ, and, with some few intervals, raged during the first three centuries, until it finally ceased, A.D. 311, by an edict of Galerius. That emperor was dying of a frightful and incurable disease, which neither physicians nor Pagan idols could alleviate. Having sent to the Christians to request them to pray for him, he issued the edict referred to, which closed the Pagan persecution of Christianity in the Roman empire. During this

* Keyster's "Travels in Germany," quoted in Macfarlane's "Catacombs of Rome."

† M. Perret has been engaged six years in these researches. Vide *Athenæum*, No. 1250, Oct., 1851.

period of persecution, they were likewise used as places of sepulture for those Christians who resided in them, as well as, doubtless, for many who, aboveground, died in the faith of Christ.

Upon the issue of the edict of Galerius, and the profession of Christianity by Constantine, which almost immediately followed, a great change necessarily took place as it regarded the use of the Catacombs. No longer a proscribed and persecuted race, the Christians came forth from their hiding-places, enjoyed the light and breathed the pure air of heaven; while those who henceforth visited the Catacombs, did so from a feeling of veneration for the martyrs and holy men whose bodies were there interred; and with a degree of superstition, easily accounted for, worshipped at their tombs in the Catacomb chapels, surrounded by the remains of the Christian dead; or they sought a grave for those whom they loved among the resting-places of those persecuted Christians, whom they regarded with so much veneration. We shall be prepared, then, to meet with two classes of monuments in our search: those which were deposited by the defenceless Christians during the first three centuries; and those which were placed in the Catacombs, after the toleration of Christianity, by those who visited them, to decorate the tombs and chapels in honour of the martyrs. Among the first we shall expect to find much which speaks of a pure, primitive, uncorrupted faith; and we must not be surprised to find occasionally among the latter some indications of that declension from primitive faith and practice which distinguished the era of the Church's worldly prosperity, and which became so apparent and marked in the succeeding centuries.

The establishment of Christianity at Rome was soon

followed by the irruption of those barbarous hordes who
overthrew the ancient city, ROME. In their search after
treasure, they ransacked the graves of the Catacombs, so
far as they were accessible, and from this period they became deserted ; all knowledge of their windings being lost,
except to banditti, thieves, and debtors, who resorted to
and made them a terror to the peaceful and well-disposed.

War, civil commotion, and social discord continued at
Rome for many centuries. The entrances to the Catacombs became lost by the falling in of the earth, the
growth of trees and rank vegetation ; from time to time,
some of them were also closed up with masonry, to prevent the galleries being used by robbers or conspirators
against the government.

About the middle of the sixteenth century, say about
a thousand years from the period of their being used as
Christian cemeteries, interest being excited concerning
them and their contents, many of them were again opened
and explored. About the year 1535, under Pope Paul
III., some of the Catacombs were cleared of rubbish,
cleansed, and lighted up. At this time, a controversy,
respecting relics, was waging in the Romish Church, and
much attention was consequently directed to the contents
of the rediscovered Catacombs. Antiquarians pursued
their inquiries with intense interest. Bosio, an Italian,
spent *more than thirty years*—from the year 1567 to 1600—
in exploring the galleries, collecting antiquities, and copy-
ing inscriptions, paintings, etc. He died while completing
his great work called *Roma Sotterranea* (Subterranean
Rome), published after his death, and translated into
Latin by Aringhi.

In 1720, another valuable work was published by
Boldetti, on the subject of the contents of the Cata-

combs; this indefatigable explorer also spent more than
thirty years of his life in these underground investiga-
tions. Bosio and Boldetti were followed by others in this
branch of study, such as Bottari, Marangoni, and Fabretti,
Italians; and MM. d'Agincourt and Raoul Rochette,
Frenchmen : the former of whom repaired to Rome to
spend *six months* in the study, but found it at once so
attractive and so vast, that he remained there *fifty years,*
and died while arranging his materials for a work published
after his death.

All these works, written either in a foreign or dead
language, and accessible only to those who could resort to
public libraries, are little known to Englishmen; gratitude is due therefore to Dr. Charles Maitland for making
the subject accessible to us by the publication, in our own
language, of his learned and deeply interesting work,
" The Church in the Catacombs."*

" It is difficult," says that writer, " now to realize the
impressions which must have been made upon the first
explorers of this subterranean city ; a vast necropolis, rich
in the bones of saints and martyrs; a stupendous testimony to the truth of Christian history, and, consequently,
to that of Christianity itself; a faithful record of the trials
of a persecuted Church. * * * * We must now
have recourse to the museums of Rome and the works of
antiquarians to understand the appearance of the Catacombs at that time, from the removal of everything
portable to a place of greater security and more easy
access, as well as from the difficulty of personally examining these dangerous galleries."

* "The Church in the Catacombs ; a Description of the Primitive Church of Rome, illustrated from Sepulchral Remains."
Longman & Co., London.

The monuments, inscriptions, and antiquities removed from the Catacombs are chiefly deposited in the Vatican Museum at Rome. The Christian Museum there contains many sarcophagi, bas-reliefs, inscriptions, and medals; but the most valuable collection of inscriptions is that of the Lapidarian Gallery, or Gallery of Stones, a long corridor in that museum, the sides of which are completely lined with slabs plastered to the walls. There is a marked contrast, however, between the two walls of this corridor and the emotions which they are calculated to excite in the minds of the thoughtful. On the right hand are arranged *Pagan* inscriptions; while opposite to them, appear more than three thousand epitaphs of the ancient and primitive *Christians.*

" I have spent," says Raoul Rochette, " many entire days in this sanctuary of antiquity, where the sacred and profane stand facing each other in the written monuments preserved to us, as in the days when Paganism and Christianity, striving with all their powers, were engaged in mortal conflict. And were it only for the treasure of impressions which we receive from this immense collection of Christian epitaphs, taken from the graves of the Catacombs and now affixed to the walls of the Vatican, this alone would be an inexhaustible fund of recollections and enjoyment for a whole life."*

The inscriptions in this and the adjoining museums are the witnesses which I shall call to testify to the Paganism of the past and the Christianity of the present, during the remainder of this course.

It must not be concluded, however, that the three thousand inscriptions of the Lapidarian Gallery are all the inscriptions which have been preserved to us. Seventy

* Raoul Rochette, " Tableau des Catacombs," p. 10.

thousand are estimated to have been contained in the Catacombs, and removed or copied at different times,* and many hundreds have been very recently discovered.

The inscriptions are chiefly upon slabs of stone or marble, used to close the graves in the walls of the galleries before referred to. Here are representations which will convey good ideas of the graves and slabs.

[81.] In one grave the skeleton is almost entire; in the other, a little dust alone remains, reminding us of the sentence pronounced upon our perishing bodies: " Dust thou art, and unto dust shalt thou return."

The inscription reads upon the upper grave :—

VALERIA SLEEPS IN PEACE.

On the lower slab the palm-branch of triumph is rudely scratched.

The slabs average generally from one to three feet in length; the letters upon them are from half an inch to four inches in height, and are scratched or cut in the stone, and the indentation usually filled in with Venetian red.

You will easily distinguish, among the illustrations which I shall exhibit to you, the *fac-similes*, or exact representations, from those which are mere *copies* of inscriptions, by noticing the rude and irregular forms of the letters in the former.

I have thus drawn a picture of Paganism ; have endeavoured to describe to you Christianity as it was introduced by its Founder—the Christianity of the New Testament. I have taken you down into the hiding-place of some of its earliest professors; I must defer to a future lecture some explanations of inscriptions and signs, which would,

* Maitland, p. 16.

without such explanation, be to you mysterious and unin-
teresting; but I desire to point out to you a *contrast*
which those silent witnesses, the tombstones of the early
Christians, enable us to draw between the two systems
called Pagan and Christian.

In nothing is the contrast between the two systems
so striking as in the *spirit in which death is regarded by
the professors of the two faiths :* with the Pagan it is extinction of existence, the termination of all that is desirable, and a feeling of disappointment or revenge is
manifested against the Great Disposer of life and death;
with the Christian all is peace, hope, anticipation of
happiness, and indication of triumph. It has been well
said, " turn where you will in the Catacombs, all is PEACE,
PEACE, PEACE, everywhere."

Let me take a few Pagan and Christian epitaphs to
illustrate this observation.   [**89.**]

Pagan.	*Christian.*
I, PROCOPE, LIFT UP MY HANDS	(Fragment.)
AGAINST GOD, WHO SNATCHED ME	WHO GAVE AND HATH TAKEN
AWAY INNOCENT. SHE LIVED	.....BLESSED.....OF THE LORD
TWENTY YEARS. PROCLUS SET UP	.....WHO LIVED—YEARS....:.
THIS.	IN PEACE, IN THE CONSULATE OF

Here the Pagan inscription regards death as an injury,
calling for resentment against God; and man's puny arm
is raised against the Great Arbiter of the universe. The
Christian epitaph, although a fragment, speaks a different
language—that of implicit submission, resignation, and
peace. "The remainder," says Dr. Maitland, "of this
inscription has been destroyed, as far as perishable marble is concerned; but the immortal sentiment which
pervades the sentence supplies the loss. Like a voice
from among the graves, broken by sobs, yet distinctly

intelligible, fall the words upon the ear :* 'The Lord
gave, and the Lord hath taken away, blessed be the
name of the Lord.'"

We are reminded by this early Christian tombstone
of a practice, which has become common in our Christian
graveyards, of inscribing texts upon tombs :—

> "His name, his years, spelt by th' unletter'd muse,
> The place of fame and elegy supply:
> And many a holy text around she strews,
> To teach the rustic moralist to die."

Again ; contrast the following inscriptions :— [**89.**]

Pagan.	*Christian.*
CAIUS JULIUS MAXIMUS, (AGED) II YEARS AND V MONTHS.	PETRONIA, A DEACON'S WIFE, THE TYPE OF MODESTY.
O RELENTLESS FORTUNE, WHO DELIGHTEST IN CRUEL DEATH, WHY IS MAXIMUS SO SUDDENLY SNATCHED FROM ME? HE WHO LATELY USED TO LIE JOYFUL ON MY BOSOM. THIS STONE NOW MARKS HIS TOMB. BEHOLD HIS MOTHER.	IN THIS PLACE I LAY MY BONES; SPARE YOUR TEARS, DEAR HUSBAND AND DAUGHTERS, AND BELIEVE THAT IT IS FORBIDDEN TO WEEP FOR ONE WHO LIVES IN GOD. BURIED IN PEACE ON THE THIRD BEFORE THE NONES OF OCTOBER, IN THE CON- SULATE OF FESTUS.

In the Pagan inscription is heard the voice of repining
and despondency; the mother weeping for her child,
"and will not be comforted, because he is not." In the
Christian epitaph, all this is reversed; the mourning
husband and daughters are consoled by the conviction
that the deceased *"lives in God,"* and are called upon to
dry their tears, under the assurance—as it is beautifully
expressed, both on the tomb and by the Apostle—that

* Maitland's " Church in the Catacombs," p. 14.

the Christian should not weep as those Pagans who have no hope of immortality. "But I would not have you to be ignorant, brethren, concerning them which are asleep, *that ye sorrow not, even as others which have no hope.* For if we believe that Jesus died and rose again, even so them also *which sleep in Jesus* will God bring with Him."*

Where can a stronger contrast in sentiment be found than exists between the Pagan and Christian monuments upon this point? Paganism, notwithstanding the allusions of her poets to Elysian fields beyond the dark waters of the Styx, had no certain hope of immortality; out of many thousands of epitaphs still extant in cabinets and museums, not one well-authenticated allusion to a settled conviction of immortality can be found.† Cicero, writing to a friend suffering from bereavement, hesitates to suggest consolation arising out of the belief in the immortality of the soul; all he can say is, "though we may *conjecture* something respecting this immortality, it is a subject *so completely in doubt,* that I dare not present it to you as a real and genuine subject of consolation."

An epitaph given by Dr. Maitland shows how the Pagan prospect was bounded by this earth, and life was looked upon as a drama which, when acted out, ended all. It reads:—

* 1 Thess. iv. 13, 14.

† In a work, published as these sheets were issuing from the press, "The Free Church of Ancient Christendom," by Basil H. Cooper, B.A., this statement is abundantly confirmed. "The author has not lighted upon a single clear example of the kind, amongst the selection of upwards of 750 sepulchral marbles given in the work of Zell; nor has he met with one such of undoubted and purely heathen origin in the only portion of Böckh's great work, the 'Corpus Inscriptionum Græcorum,' tom. i.—iii." (p. 17, note.)

WHILE I LIVED, I LIVED   WELL. MY DRAMA IS NOW ENDED: SOON YOURS
WILL BE. FAREWELL, AND APPLAUD ME.

How different the sentiment of the following, from the
Catacombs, in which the separate existence and happiness
of the soul are regarded as certainties :—

NICEPHORUS, A SWEET SOUL IN REFRESHMENT.

Again :—

LAURENCE TO HIS SWEETEST SON SEVERUS, THE WELL-DESERVING, BORNE
AWAY BY ANGELS ON THE VIITH BEFORE THE IDES OF JANUARY.

The same idea is beautifully illustrated by the following inscription on the tomb of a martyr, who suffered
under the Antonine persecution, which commenced about
the year A.D. 160. The original is decorated with the
monogram of Christ, and olive-branch, and also exhibits
a pot containing fire—perhaps referring to the manner of
his death :—

ALEXANDER IS NOT DEAD, BUT LIVES ABOVE THE STARS, AND HIS BODY
RESTS IN THIS TOMB. HE ENDED LIFE UNDER THE EMPEROR ANTONINE,
WHO, FORESEEING THAT GREAT BENEFIT WOULD RESULT FROM HIS SER-
VICES, RETURNED EVIL FOR GOOD. FOR WHILE ON HIS KNEES AND ABOUT
TO SACRIFICE TO THE TRUE GOD, HE WAS LED AWAY TO EXECUTION.
OH, SAD TIMES! IN WHICH, AMONG SACRED RITES AND PRAYERS, EVEN
IN CAVERNS, WE ARE NOT SAFE.   WHAT CAN BE MORE WRETCHED THAN
SUCH A LIFE? AND WHAT THAN SUCH A DEATH? WHEN THEY CANNOT BE
BURIED BY THEIR FRIENDS AND RELATIONS. AT LENGTH THEY SPARKLE
IN HEAVEN. HE HAS SCARCELY LIVED, WHO HAS LIVED IN CHRISTIAN
TIMES.

Respecting this interesting monument, Dr. Maitland
remarks: " ' He lives above the stars, and his body rests
in this tomb ;' there is faith in this joining together, as

things equally tangible and matter of fact, the place of
his spiritual abode, and the resting-place of his body.
There are also other points in the inscription worthy of
notice.   The first words, 'Alexander is dead,' after leading us to expect a lamentation, break out into an assurance of glory and immortality; the description of the
temporal insecurity in which the believers of that time
lived; the difficulty of procuring Christian burial for the
martyrs, with the certainty of their heavenly reward; and
the concluding sentence forcibly recalling the words of
St. Paul—'as dying, and behold we live.'"* Truly
these inscriptions throw more light than all the Commen-
taries upon one passage of Scripture:—"*Christ hath
brought life and immortality to light through the Gospel.*"†
   In another respect, the Pagan and Christian inscriptions, standing face to face, in the Lapidarian Gallery, are
most illustrative of the two religions of which they are
the silent exponents.   On the Pagan side is found a proud
array of names.   The *nomen, prænomen,* and *cognomen;*
and of titles, hereditary, imperial, civil, military, and mu-
nicipal.   "Further on, the whole heaven of Paganism is
glorified by innumerable altars, where the epithets, 'un-
conquered, greatest, and best,' are lavished upon the
worthless shadows that peopled Olympus.   The first
glance at the opposite wall is enough to show, that 'not
many mighty, not many noble,' were numbered among
those whose epitaphs are there displayed; that these
records, in almost every instance, are 'the short and
simple annals of the poor.'   The Christian convert deemed
it sufficient to be recognized by that name which belonged
to him as a subject of the heavenly kingdom."   "Till the
number of Christians increased so as to render a further

* Maitland's "Church in the Catacombs," p 40.   † 2 Tim. i. 10.

distinction necessary, the Christian name alone was recorded in the cemetery."*

Witness the following simple inscriptions :—

THE PLACE OF PHILEMON.

VIRCINIUS REMAINED BUT A SHORT TIME WITH US.

THE PLACE OF SEVUS.

MARTYRIA, IN PEACE.

THE DORMITORY OF ELPIS.

PRIMA, PEACE BE TO THEE.

ZOTICUS LAID HERE TO SLEEP.

CEMELLA SLEEPS IN PEACE.

And now you will agree with me that it is high time
that I bring my lecture to some practical conclusion.
Allow me, for a minute, to recall the subjects we have
been considering, before I attempt to deduce the improvement of which they are susceptible.

We spoke of the doubts and gloomy forebodings of
human nature, groping, in the midst of "darkness which
might be felt," for light and hope of deliverance. I told
you of intense desire and high anticipation of coming
help from above. I pointed out to you the fulfilment of
all hopes and anticipations in the rising of "the Sun of
Righteousness, with healing in His wings;" the advent
of "a light to them which sat in darkness and the shadow
of death, to guide their footsteps into the way of peace."
I contrasted the teaching of this Deliverer with the

* Maitland's "Church in the Catacombs," pp. 12, 15.

Pagan teaching of old. I spoke of His new and startling doctrine spreading even to Rome, the world's capital. I hinted briefly at its rough reception there, and the cruel treatment of its unoffending professors; of the victory which their steadfast faith and patient endurance wrought over the powers of the earth. You accompanied me to view their ancient underground dwellings, used as hiding-places, churches, and "*sleeping-places.*"* We together explored their dark and winding galleries, noticed their tombs and inscriptions, by which they told the simple tale of confiding faith and unshaken hope in a crucified Lord and Master; their conviction of union with Him, and "sure and certain hope" of a resurrection from the dead.

And what do we learn from all this?

I would have you notice, if you have not done so already, *the irresistible, the stupendous power of pure Christianity; and*, noticing that, ask yourselves if it be not *of Divine origin?*

Reflect, for a few moments, on the state of the contending parties and systems at Rome, in mortal conflict, during the occupation of the Catacombs. On the one side were arrayed *all the powers of the world*—the Roman emperors, whose will dictated law to the earth; a powerful army; all the wealth of Rome; all the learning of the Augustan period; all the intellect of philosophy and science "falsely so called;" a priesthood, whose influence extended to the bounds of the Roman empire, and whose power perhaps exceeded even that of the emperor himself; all the rulers; the great majority of the people; and the *prestige* of high antiquity in favour of a religion which was admirably adapted to the human heart.

* The name "cemetery," *i.e.*, *sleeping-place,* was first used by the Christians of the Catacombs.

On the other side we find a few poor, illiterate, despised outcasts, hiding in "dens and caves of the earth," without arms, or refusing to use them ; decimated by persecutions repeated again and again ; opposing their enemies, not with carnal weapons, but blessing and praying for them ; and yet we find one emperor after another declaring that they were "*incorrigible*," or, in other words, *invincible*.

Again and again edicts went forth to exterminate them from the earth ; and inscriptions were set up to celebrate and perpetuate the supposed success of the persecutions. Here are two which have been preserved by antiquarian writers :—

DIOCLETIAN, CÆSAR, AUGUSTUS, HAVING ADOPTED GALERIUS IN THE EAST ; THE SUPERSTITION OF THE CHRISTIANS BEING EVERYWHERE DESTROYED, AND THE WORSHIP OF THE GODS PROPAGATED.

Again :—

DIOCLETIAN, JOVIUS, AND MAXIMIAN, HERCULEUS, CÆSAR, AUGUSTUS. THE ROMAN EMPIRE HAVING BEEN ENLARGED THROUGHOUT THE EAST AND THE WEST, AND THE NAME OF THE CHRISTIANS, WHO WERE OVERTHROWING THE ROMAN REPUBLIC, BLOTTED OUT. *

Never in the world's history was there found a more striking instance of the short-sightedness of man, and the irresistible working of the providence of God. Within ten years from the reign of Diocletian, the " *superstition everywhere destroyed*," and the "*name blotted out*," became the prevailing, the established religion of the Roman Empire. The seed cast into the ground, imbued from the first with Divine life, and watered con-

---

* According to Gruter, these inscriptions were found upon two columns in Spain. They are quoted in Neander's "General

tinually by the Divine blessing, sprang all at once into observation, asserting its power, and overturning the decaying system which impeded for a time its upward progress.

But you may object, perhaps,—If Christianity is Divine, why did it not arrive earlier in the world ? To this I must reply very briefly, that God is Sovereign : " He doeth as He will in the armies of heaven, and among the inhabitants of the earth." No one may reasonably say unto Him, " What doest Thou ? "

But, beyond this general reply, I think there are reasons apparent why the coming of Christ was delayed.

I would ask you, was there no wisdom displayed in delaying Divine help until man had proved to his heart's content his own *helplessness ?*

Man is so proud, so self-sufficient, that surely it was befitting that he should try a religion of his own—should

Church History," i. 210. In the original language they are as follow :—

DIOCLETIAN . CÆS.
AVG. . GALERIO . IN . ORI
ENTE . ADOPT. . SVPERS
TITIONE . CHRIST.
VBIQ. . DELETA . ET . CVL
TV . DEOR. . PROPAGATO.

———

DIOCLETIANVS . IOVIVS . ET
MAXIMIAN . HERCVLEVS .
CÆS. . AVG.
AMPLIFICATO . PER . ORIENTEM . OCCIDENTEM .
IMP. . ROM. .
ET
NOMINE . CHRISTIANORVM .
DELETO . QUI .
REMP. . EVER
TEBANT.

be filled with his own devices, before interference in his behalf was attempted. Do we not so deal with the self-willed among ourselves? "Let them go their own way," say we, "try their own remedies; and, when they discover that they require help, they will gladly accept it." I do think, my friends, that when a few more thousand years have rolled away—and with God they are but as one day—that all will admit that the troubled infancy of this world, its moral disorder, and its yearnings for order and peace, will not have been without their uses; as the chaotic upbreakings of the earth's physical surface in past ages are now ministering to our wants, our comfort, and to human advancement. I could, if time permitted, show you that the period selected for the mission of Christ was admirably adapted for the purpose contemplated: in that the world had come to be under the rule of *one* emperor, whose policy tolerated all religions, so that Christianity was carried, in its early days, even to the burning sands of India and to the snows of Siberia; in that the Jewish Scriptures and prophecies had been translated into Greek, and the literature of that polished nation had been extensively diffused over the world; in that the troubles which had fallen upon Palestine had distributed the Jews into "every nation under heaven." All these circumstances concurred to further the spread of Christianity, while they indicated that the "fulness of time had come."

Or you may, some of you, perhaps object—If Christianity was from God, why did it not cast down Paganism at once and destroy it on the spot?

God does not work so, either in the moral or the physical world. The earthquake and the tornado are not His *usual* but His *extraordinary* agencies. *Why* He does not so work is not for us to determine; we can watch, however, and trace His working in Nature, and we shall find it agree with His dealings in Providence. God is in no haste (if I may use the expression). His time is not limited like man's, who, if he have aught to do, must "do it with all his might," for "the night cometh when no man can work." But it is not so with God; eternity is before Him, and He works, to our senses, *deliberately, but surely and irresistibly.*

Let us consider an illustration of His method of working.

Insignificant insects are diligently piling atom upon atom; ages pass away, and their work is gradually rising to the top of the waters, lifting up itself *a coral reef* above the foaming waves; sea-birds alight on it, and sea-weed is flung upon it, and contribute to the formation of a soil; volcanic action, deep seated beneath, is heaving gradually the surface into hill and dale. A bird drops a seed here, a wave casts up another there. The graceful palm, the useful bread-fruit, and the grateful orange spring up, and a forest diversifies the scene.

But thousands of years have passed away since the animalcules began their task.

Look again: a drifted canoe is borne out of its accustomed course; the island is peopled; the inhabitants are naked, savage, idolatrous, bloodthirsty. Another thousand years wing their flight.

Again the scene changes: a strange sail is in sight, a boat puts off—civilized men are landing; they make overtures of peace and of reciprocal barter. The inhabitants clothe themselves, and erect convenient dwellings; a written language is being constructed. A printing-press is set up; the Book of Truth is printed, read, acted upon. They have "cast their idols to the moles and to the bats;" they have thrown down their blood-stained altars; they have converted their "swords into ploughshares, and their spears into pruning-hooks." GOD'S PURPOSE IS COMPLETE; *but it has occupied perhaps six thousand years to bring it about.*

Count not, then, God's years as you would number the few days allotted to yourselves. "The Lord is not slack as men count slackness." Let us beware of attempting to measure with our puny lines the depths of infinity and the length and breadth of eternity, remembering that

> ——"His judgments are a mighty deep,
> Where plummet of archangel's intellect
> Could never yet find soundings, but from age
> To age, let down, drawn up, then thrown again,
> With lengthened line and added weight, yet fails:
> For still the cry in heaven is, ' *Oh, the depth!* '"

Learn, then, that when God works none may hinder Him, but He will work like an Eternal God nevertheless. Thus worked He, and thus works He still, with regard to CHRISTIANITY, the Divinely-appointed agency for this world's regeneration. It has cast down the Paganism of the Roman Empire; it is now at work upon other evils to which I must refer in my concluding lecture. In the words of our Lord's parable, the leaven cast into the meal is at work, "until the whole is leavened." It is actively engaged upon Eastern and Western Paganism, and is undermining and supplanting false religion and superstition all over the world.

> ——————"Its wakening smiles
> Have broke the gloom of Pagan sleep;
> The Word has reached the utmost isles;
> God's spirit moves upon the deep.

Already, from the dust of death,
Man, in his Maker's image, stands;
Once more he draws immortal breath,
And stretches forth to heaven his hands."

In conclusion, *let me bespeak your gratitude* for what Christianity has done for us. It would have done more, but for the reasons I shall assign in my last lecture; but its beneficial effects are too apparent not to demand grateful acknowledgment.

Paganism amongst us has been cast out, with its cruelty, human sacrifices, and revolting rites. The horrors of war have been mitigated. In lieu of child-murder, carried on systematically, we have asylums for mothers in the hour of trial, for foundlings, orphans, the ragged, the starving and the forsaken. Mercy is now extended to the poor, the outcast, and the abandoned. We have refuges for the erring, the idiot, and the de-mented; hospitals for the wounded, the sick, and the dying. Suicide and revenge, once accounted honourable, are now disgraceful and illegal. Woman has been lifted to the level she was designed to occupy; instead of the drudge and slave of man, she is now, with us, his equal, the ornament and the happiness of his home. And with respect to yourselves, as forming part of the great mass of the people, how has Christianity improved your posi-tion, your moral character!

Had you lived in those days of Pagan darkness, how would you, my friends, have amused yourselves this evening? Instead of listening to a lecture, which, by your attention, I conclude, has been interesting, you would, in all probability, with your families, have been gloating over scenes of bloodshed, or indulging unfeel-ing ears with the cries and groans of the helpless, the

wounded, and the dying ; have been shouting, perchance,
for " The Christians to the lions !" or would have rioted,
perhaps, because some fresh victim, to be torn with the
*ungulæ,** had been denied to you. You and I, but for
God's grace, might have been equally callous to human
suffering with human nature of old ; and this very evening we might have given, again and again, the signal to
despatch a fellow-mortal, already so miserable, that death
would hardly be regarded as a foe. Or, if illuminated
by the light of the Gospel shining in our hearts, you and
I might have occupied the more enviable position as victims, to make sport for a short hour for all ranks and
classes of Pagan Rome.

You will remind me that *slavery* is still practised in
some countries by professing Christians, attended by
many of its most revolting features. I have not forgotten it ; *who could ignore the painful fact ?* The inconsistency is so glaring, that it is difficult to determine
whether feelings of astonishment or of shame predominate
in the breast of the Christian who regards it. The opponent of Christianity may well point his finger at such an
exhibition ; but I must beg his candid attention to one
or two statements, which he in fairness must listen to
before he comes to a decision hostile to Christianity,
founded on such inconsistency.

No sooner had Christianity attained to worldly power,
than it directed itself to mitigate evils which it could
not immediately subdue. The manumission—that is,
liberation—of slaves, was esteemed so honourable in the
Christian, that the first Christian emperor dignified the

* Instruments of iron, resembling a claw or hand, used for
tearing and lacerating the flesh.

act by requiring that their emancipation should be announced *by the bishop before the assembled Church.* Many honours have been, since that day, bestowed upon Church dignitaries by the powers of the earth. What higher dignity than this could be conferred by them on a minister of Jesus Christ?

The institution of slavery fell throughout Europe, not with a sudden crash, but gradually, before the advance and extension of Christianity. No one can put his finger on the period and say, *"* Then and there ended slavery ;*" but slavery, in Western Christian Europe at least, is extinct.* In the Augustan age, out of twenty-eight millions of Europeans, at least half of that number are estimated to have groaned under the most cruel bondage. Athens, the most refined city in the world— *the boasted home of freedom*—at the height of her prosperity, *possessed* 421,000 *inhabitants,* 400,000 *of whom were slaves.*† Of the numerical predominance of slaves over freemen at Rome, I have already spoken. Where are they now? If you travel from the Pillars of Hercules to the Danube, from the Icy Cape to the foot of Italy, not one is to be found. We can afford to bear with the taunt of the opponent of Christianity, having such a fact to appeal to; but I have another to point out no less conclusive.

Christianity, as you will learn, kept not its first estate. The fine gold became dim, and many of the old evils crept back to afflict mankind; amongst them slavery,

* This Lecture was delivered before the abolition of serfdom in the Russian Empire, by which 25,000,000 serfs, who had neither wives, children, or property to call their own, were liberated in the year 1862.

† Lecture by Professor Alison, on the "Influence of Christianity." London : Seeleys, 1852.

like a bird of evil omen, scented the corruption, and returned to its congenial pursuits. The slave-trade with Africa sprang up, and a legalized traffic in flesh and blood was carried on by many nations professing Christianity. Not, however, to be acquiesced in silently, as to Pagan times; the advocates of the wrong were doomed to listen to the murmurs, the complaints, and, afterwards, the indignant declamation, the withering denunciation, of Christian patriots and statesmen. The Statute 3 & 4 William IV., chapter 73, was the proud result, passed on the 28th August, 1833. By this Act, slavery, previously unlawful in Britain, became illegal throughout her vast dominions. Let me request you to bear in mind this statute—as Englishmen you may well indulge an honest pride that you can identify yourselves with such a measure. It furnishes a striking comment on the power of Christianity. A nation taxing itself voluntarily, almost unanimously, to the amount of twenty millions of pounds, in order that it might be for ever free from the crime of slavery, conferred upon itself, by that act, more real dignity and glory than it acquired by its conquests by sea and land—all its accumulated triumphs of science, literature, and commerce.

Slavery is now repudiated by all the European States (Spain excepted), and treaties of mutual co-operation exist between them for its prevention. It requires not the prophet's vision to foretell its *early downfall* elsewhere; its chains are loosening, its yoke is falling from the neck, before the silent but irresistible force of Christian opinion. Whether its abettors will have the wisdom to perceive their peril and avert their own ruin, or whether they will be involved in the coming destruction of slavery, is for themselves to determine by timely action.

*As certainly as the sun rising dispels the midnight vapours,
so certainly will the extending doctrine of the " Sun of
Righteousness " proclaim " liberty to the captive, and the
opening of the prison to them that are bound."* *

If Christianity has effected such changes in the habits,
tastes, and condition of men; if it has accomplished all
that I have indicated in this lecture—and my conscience
acquits me of having at all overstated its results—then
I would say, in conclusion, do not let us lightly reject its
claims to be Divine, or be ungrateful for what it has
already effected. Rather let us evince our gratitude by
studying more earnestly its character, and drinking more
deeply of its spirit, depending unhesitatingly upon its
power to accomplish ultimately *all that it came to perform.*

* This was first written in 1851. The fall of slavery in the
United States, predicted as above, was, in the good providence
of God, accomplished as a result of the Civil War by which the
blind advocates of slavery destroyed themselves, and brought
about the liberation of four millions of slaves. The Constitu-
tional Amendment abolishing slavery was ratified by the States,
and on the 18th of December, 1865, proclamation was issued accordingly. The following beautiful poem was written by J. G.
Whittier, on hearing the bells ring on that happy occasion :—

LAUS DEO !

It is done !
Clang of bell and roar of gun
Send the tidings up and down.
How the belfries rock and reel,
How the great guns, peal on peal,
Fling the joy from town to town.

Ring, O bells !
Every stroke exulting tells
Of the burial-hour of crime.
Loud and long that all may hear
Ring for every listening ear
Of Eternity and Time !

Let us kneel :
God's own voice is in that peal,
And this spot is holy ground.
Lord forgive us !   What are we,
That our eyes this glory see,
That our ears have heard the sound ?

For the Lord
On the whirlwind is abroad ;
In the earthquake He has spoken :
He has smitten with his thunder
The iron walls asunder,
And the gates of brass are broken !

Loud and long,
Lift the old exulting song ;
Sing with Miriam by the sea :
He hath cast the mighty down ;
Horse and rider sink and drown ;
He hath triumphed gloriously !

Did we dare
In our agony of prayer
Ask for more than He has done ?
When was ever his right hand
Over any time or land
Stretched as now beneath the sun !

How they pale,
Ancient myth, and song, and tale,
In this wonder of our days,
When the cruel rod of war
Blossoms white with righteous law,
And the wrath of man is praise !

Blotted out !
All within and all about
Shall a fresher life begin ;
Freer breathe the universe
As it rolls its heavy curse
On the dead and buried sin !

It is done !
In the circuit of the sun
Shall the sound thereof go forth.
It shall bid the sad rejoice,
It shall give the dumb a voice,
It shall belt with joy the earth !

Ring and swing
Bells of joy ! on morning's wing
Send the song of praise abroad :
With a sound of broken chains
Tell the nations that He reigns
Who alone is Lord and God !

LECTURE III.

THE CATACOMBS.

"'They wandered in dens and caves of the earth."—Heb. xi. 38.

My last lecture extended to such length, that I was constrained to postpone mention of many interesting points connected with the Catacombs. I propose bringing them before you this evening, previously to replying to a common objection, which must occupy our attention during the remainder of our course.

When you call to memory the statement of the Apostle Paul,* that " not many wise (learned) men after the flesh, not many mighty, not many noble were called," to profess Christianity, you will be prepared to hear that the inscriptions of the Catacombs are not to be studied as models of classic elegance ; on the contrary, they are often rude in the extreme, and betray ignorance of letters in those who dictated, as well as in those who executed the work.

In one case the inscription has been entirely reversed, excepting the letter n, so that it must be spelt backward to make sense of it. It is an epitaph set up to Elia Vincentia, the wife of Virginius ; the husband, if living, must have been unable to read, and he does not appear to have had any friend capable of pointing out the blunder.

* 1 Cor. i. 26.

Orthography, or spelling, is generally found very defective, and the grammar is often as bad as the spelling, and consequently the meaning is frequently difficult to determine. B is very commonly put for V. One specimen will suffice for an example. [82.]

The inscription, of which I show you a fac-simile, reads thus :

SABINI BISO
MUM SE BIBUM
FECIT SIBI IN CYMI
IERIUM BᴿAᶠIBINAE
IN CRYPTA NOBA.

The meaning is, " The bisomum (grave for two) of Sabinus; he made it for himself during his lifetime, in the cemetery of Balbina, in the new crypt."

Here *b* is put for *v* in *bibum*, *um* is put for *o* as the termination of that word, which should be *vivo*; *cemeterio* is spelt *cymiierium*; *balbinæ* had been spelt correctly, excepting that the *l* is upside down, but some ill-informed critic has interpolated an *r* and an *f*, which has made matters worse; while in the last word *nova*, the *v* is again displaced by a *b*. I shall not dwell longer upon the literary part of the subject, as more important and interesting matter demands our attention. I will only observe, that words dictated in Greek are often found written in Roman letters, while Roman words are sometimes written in Greek letters, and occasionally the languages are oddly mixed.

Thus : PRIMA IRENE SOE is Greek couched in Latin letters, meaning " Prima, peace to thee."

It does not appear to have been a general practice to

SABINI BISO
MUMSEBIBUM
FECITSIBIINCYMI
JERIUMBAFIBINAE
INCRYPTANOBA

EMPTVM·LOCVM·A·BARTEMISTVM
VISOMVM·HOC·EST·ET·PRETIVM
DATVM·A·FOSSORI·HILARO·ID·EST

FOLÑ ⋈⃝ PRESENTIA
SEVERI
FOSS·ET·LAVRENT

DIOGENES·FOSSOR·IN·PACE·DEPOSITVS
OCTABV·KALENDAS·OCTOBRIS

82

A FOSSOR — WITH INSCRIPTION.

NABIRA IN PACE ANIMA DVLCIS
QVI BIXIT ANOS +·XVI·M·V·
ANIMA MELEIEA
TITVLV FACTV
APARENTES SIGNVM
NABE

PONTIVS·LEO·S·EBIV
ET PONTIA·M·
FECERVNT·FI

IVLIO FILIO PATER DOLIENS.

PORCELLA HIC
DORMIT IN P·QVIXIT
ANN·III·M·X·D·XIII·

83

SYMBOLS RELATING TO NAMES.

place dates upon the gravestones; many of them, however, give the names of the Roman Consuls in office, by
which names the date can be ascertained, as lists of the
Consuls have been preserved to our times. The earliest
slab containing the consular date appears to have been
set up A.D. 98—that is, about sixty-one years from the
death of Christ; the next is dated A.D. 102, about the
period of the death of the beloved Apostle John; another
is inscribed A.D. 111; and others, various dates, of the
second, third, and fourth centuries. It must not be concluded that no Christians were buried in the Catacombs
before the year 98, but that no earlier date has been left
upon record. Thousands of graves contain nothing more
than a name, and some symbol of faith in Christ and
hope in the resurrection.

A body of men existed whose office it was to construct
the graves and regulate all matters relating to interments.
They were called *fossors,* or sextons; probably they were
originally the sand-diggers and quarrymen, converted to
Christianity by witnessing its effects upon those who
professed that faith, brought as they were into close
and immediate contact with its persecuted professors and
martyrs. They became afterwards a regularly organized
body of excavators and guides, and had charge probably of the lamps which have been found in niches at
certain intervals, and not only made tombs, but sold and
conveyed them.

Here is a painting from the cemetery of Callistus.
The inscription at the top reads [**82.**]—

DIOGENES THE FOSSOR, BURIED IN PEACE ON THE EIGHTH BEFORE
THE KALENDS OF OCTOBER

In one hand he holds a pick, in the other a lamp, furnished with a spike to drive into the rock; on the ground
are his cutting implements, hammer, and compasses for
marking out the graves; the recess behind him is lined
with tombs, covered with slabs; at his feet is an open
grave; while the Greek X (Chi) on his dress, the initial
letter of Christ, indicates his Christian profession, and
the doves with olive-branches the peace in which he rests.

Here is another slab, from which we learn that the
fossors sold and conveyed the graves, and we gather
something of the prices paid for them : [**82.**]

THE PLACE BOUGHT BY BARTEMISTUS, THAT IS, A BISOMUM, AND THE
PRICE PAID TO THE FOSSOR HILARUS, THE SUM OF FOURTEEN HUNDRED
FOLLES, IN THE PRESENCE OF THE FOSSORS SEVERUS AND LAURENCE.

This perfect but very concise form of conveyance might
be studied with advantage by our modern conveyancers.
The price paid for the grave in our money would be
£1 2s. 7d.

I have told you already that not many learned were
gathered to Christ in the earlier ages of the Church, consequently very many could not read the inscriptions.
How, then, were friends and survivors to distinguish the
graves of those they loved and mourned ? They availed
themselves of the use of *pictures, symbols, or signs.* This
is very clear, for the connection of the symbol with the
name or trade of the person buried is easily traced in
many cases. For instance, here are four epitaphs of this
kind, each of them having some representation as a
symbol in addition to the inscription. [**83.**]

NAVIA IN PEACE,—A SWEET SOUL, WHO LIVED SIXTEEN YEARS AND
FIVE MONTHS—A SOUL SWEET AS HONEY. THIS EPITAPH WAS MADE
BY HER PARENTS—THE SIGN A SHIP.

Now *navis* is the Latin for ship, and a ship is represented as the best phonetic symbol for Navira. Again :

PONTIUS LEO MADE THIS FOR HIMSELF WHILE LIVING. HE AND HIS WIFE,
PONTIA MAXIMA, MADE THIS FOR THEIR WELL-DESERVING SON APOLLINARIS.

Here *leo* is the Latin for lion, and a lion is used accordingly to point out the tomb of Pontius Leo and his son.

Again : here are two casks, and the inscription :

DOLIENS THE FATHER TO JULIUS HIS SON.

Dolium is Latin for cask, a cask is put to symbolize
the name of Doliens.

Once more : here is an inscription with a pig, and we
find it is the tomb of a little girl named *Porcella*, which
means in Latin a little pig. It reads :

HERE SLEEPS PORCELLA IN PEACE; SHE LIVED THREE YEARS, TEN MONTHS,
THIRTEEN DAYS.

Roman Catholic writers have invented many super-
stitious stories to account for these symbols, which they
regarded as evidences of martyrdom. The spread of
learning since the last century has dispelled, however,
much of this ignorance.

It was a common practice with many nations of antiquity to represent the pursuits of life, tools, or working
implements, upon the tombs of the dead; and also to
place such articles in the graves. This accounts for many
such articles found in graves in the Catacombs, and also
for another class of symbols represented on the gravestones, referring evidently to the trades and occupations
of the deceased.

Here is a gravestone with the inscription [**84**]—

BAUTO AND MAXIMA MADE THIS DURING THEIR LIFETIME.

A saw, chisel, and adze evidently tell that a Bauto was a carpenter by trade.

Another, with two mallets and a knife, is evidently the grave of one engaged in a trade which cannot, however, be fixed with any certainty. It reads :—

CONSTANTIA, BURIED IN PEACE, ON THE LORD'S DAY THE SIXTH BEFORE THE KALENDS OF JULY, IN THE FIFTH CONSULATE OF HONORIUS AUGUSTUS WHO LIVED SIXTY YEARS, MORE OR LESS, TO THE WELL-DESERVING, IN PEACE.

The date of this grave, A.D. 402, long after the persecutions ceased, proves that the symbols had nothing to do with martyrdom.

A broken slab, with the simple inscription, THE PLACE OF ADEODATUS, has representations of the implements of a woolcomber.

Another, to VENERIA, IN PEACE, would indicate that she was in the same trade ; a very common one at Rome, where almost all classes wore woollen garments.

Another gravestone is erected to the wife of a shoemaker, two slippers being scratched thereon. The inscription, the first line of which is missing, reads [85] :

—— TWENTY-SEVEN YEARS, SIX MONTHS, ELEVEN DAYS, AND EIGHT HOURS. MARCIANUS, TO HIS MOST WORTHY WIFE, IN PEACE.

An ancient bushel-measure, filled with grain, scratched upon another stone, would seem to indicate that it closed the grave of one who dealt in corn. It reads :

VICTORINA, IN PEACE, AND IN CHRIST.

One more illustration upon the subject must suffice.

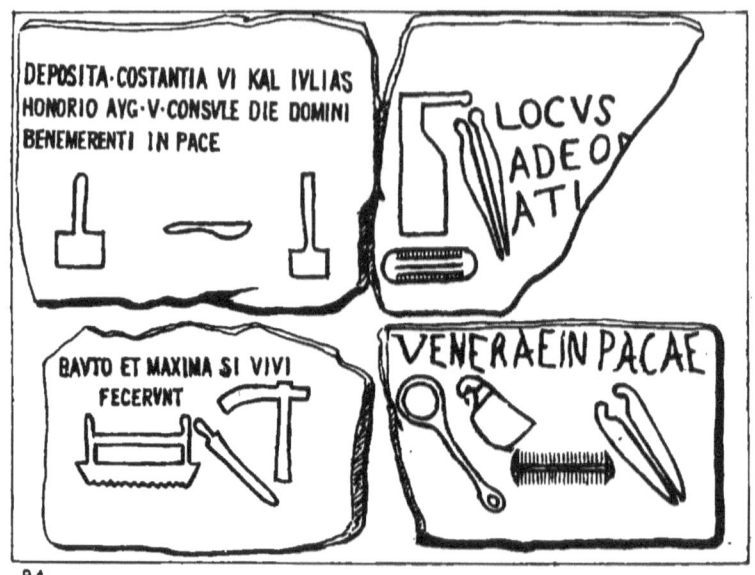

84

SYMBOLS REFERING TO OCCUPATIONS.

85

SYMBOLS REFERING TO OCCUPATIONS.

A slab represents a stonemason at work upon a sarcophagus; a boy is helping him, by working the drill employed in boring the stone; the other implements of the
trade are on the ground; and the finished sarcophagus,
with a name on it agreeing with the name in the inscription, informs us that Eutropus was engaged in the trade
of a sculptor and maker of sepulchral monuments. He
stands in a praying attitude, with a cup in his hand. The
inscription, which is in Greek, reads:

THE HOLY WORSHIPPER OF GOD, EUTROPUS, IN PEACE. HIS SON MADE
THIS. HE DIED ON THE TENTH KALENDS OF SEPTEMBER.

It would be an interesting inquiry, but beside my purpose, to ascertain how far these endeavours to inscribe,
symbolically, names and professions led to the general
adoption of family symbols, such as crests and armorial
bearings; which very commonly consist of some allusion
to or play upon the family name or occupations. This
practice— subsequently reduced into system, as the science
of heraldry—has usually been attributed to the inscribing
of symbols on the shields of those who engaged in the
Crusades in the Holy Land during the middle ages; but
it is quite evident the practice was not then originated,
but merely revived, for traces of it exist not only in the
Catacombs at Rome but upon the tombs of the Armenian
Christians to this day; it was adopted by wealthy families
in the Augustan age; by Mecænas, for instance, whose
crest was a frog, and may be detected in the graves of the
kings of Egypt, and on the cylinders and seals of ancient
Assyria.

I must now proceed to explain another and most interesting class of symbols universally prevalent in the

7

Catacombs, namely, those which relate to the *religious belief* of the early Christians.

Ignorant as they mainly were of both reading and writing, and persecuted for their faith in Christ, it was obviously necessary that some symbol should be found which should enable them to express their belief, and be at the same time unintelligible to their persecutors. Hence arose the use of two common symbols; one of which is called the Monogram (that is, one character composed of more than one letter), and the other is called the Fish. It is thought that the monogram came first into use, but its signification being discovered, it was no longer capable of shielding the Christian tombs from insult and desecration; the other more occult symbol was consequently employed.

The monogram, in its earliest form, consisted only of the two Greek letters, X (Chi) and P (Rho), the initial letters of ΧΡΙΣΤΟΣ, the Greek name of Christ. These letters were like our X and P, and we find the X with the P drawn standing within it, Thus:

Here is a rude illustration, which reads

TASARIS, IN CHRIST, THE FIRST AND THE LAST.   [86]

The monogram is here used for "Christ," and the Greek letters Alpha and Omega being added to it to express "the first and the last," as the titles of the Lord Jesus Christ, adopted by Himself in the Book of Revelation.*

Here is another example of the symbol, and also of the prevailing ignorance upon literary points. A fragment of stone containing part of a date, THE FIRST BEFORE

* Revelation i. 8, 11, etc.

THE IDES, has the monogram, with the Alpha and Omega, surrounded by a circle, which device the sculptor has represented *upside down*.

Observe also two other forms of this symbol, each of them surrounded by a circle, evidently intended to express belief in the eternity of Christ, the circle being a significant and very ancient symbol of eternity in use among the ancients. In the one case the monogram is represented simply with the Alpha and Omega; in the other case, the letters E S D E I S are found encircling the monogram, which is supposed to signify *Christus est Deus* (Christ is God).

A transition from the Greek Chi to the upright cross was likely soon to be suggested, as representing symbolically the instrument of our Lord's crucifixion. This took place in course of time, and is seen frequently on more recent monuments; the head of the Rho being affixed to the upper limb of the cross. Thus:

Two instances I point out to you; one of them simple, the other enclosed in an equilateral triangle, supposed to signify the faith in the doctrine of a Triune God.*

The other symbol, which had reference to the faith in Christ, was a fish—difficult to unriddle, had it not been that inscriptions with the Greek word Ιχθυς, a fish, as well as the representation itself, occurred, pointing out that the significance rested with the *letters of the word*, as as well as with the object itself. The explanation is that the word is formed from the initials of the Greek words describing the names, titles, and office of the Lord Jesus

* This instance is derived from Twinings's "Early and Mediæval Christian Art."

Christ, viz., Ιησους Χριστος, Θεου Υιος, Σωτηρ (Jesus Christ, Son of God, the Saviour).

Here are illustrations from the Lapidarian Gallery; one of the Fish, and the other of the word ΙΧΘΥΣ, on an inscription, which reads : [87]

ΙΚ*ΘΥΣ (IN CHRIST), TO THE GOOD AND INNOCENT SON OF PASTORUS WHO LIVED X YEARS AND IIII MONTHS.

You will recollect that I referred to the fact of Jews being in Rome at the period of the introduction of Christianity there, and to the statement of Suetonius that they raised tumults respecting that faith. The concluding chapter of the Acts of the Apostles informs us of the same fact, for Paul, on his arrival at Rome,† sent for the Jews, and reasoned with them on the subject of Christianity; but finding them generally averse to its reception, he turned to the Romans, saying, "Be it known therefore unto you, that the salvation of God is sent unto the Gentiles, and that they will hear it." Now, it may be interesting to you to know that, unlikely as it may appear, the Catacombs afford evidence of this state of things; that Jews were at Rome; that, being confounded with the Christians, naturally enough they participated in their persecutions, and sought refuge with them in the Catacombs, but, nevertheless, kept themselves apart from the Christians as it regarded their religious services.

In one of the galleries on the Via Portuense, containing no Christian inscription whatever, there was found by Bosio a lamp, having on it a representation of the golden candlestick of the Temple of Jerusalem, and upon the wall over it the word SYNAGOGUE, in Greek letters,

---

* K ignorantly for X.   † Acts xxviii. 17—28.

86

RELIGIOUS SYMBOLS.

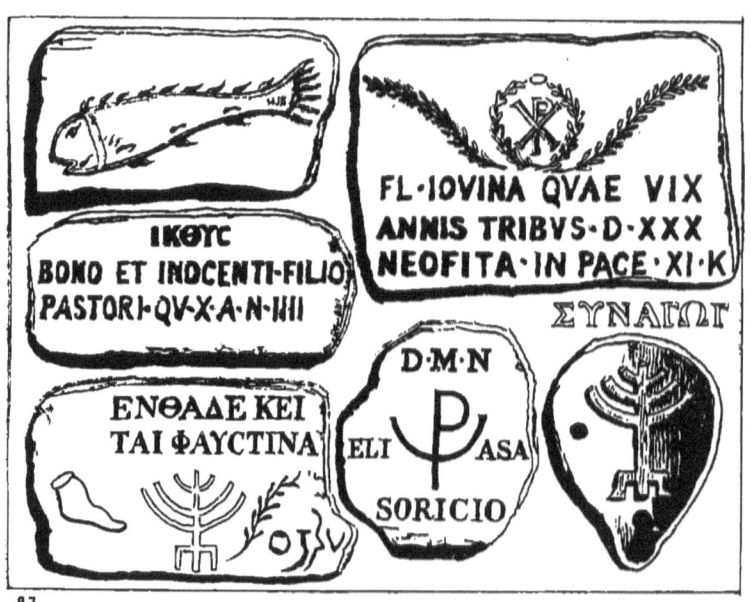

87

SUNDRY REPRESENTATIONS IN CATACOMBS.

evidently indicating the place of meeting for Jewish worship. [**87**] It is clear, notwithstanding, that some of Jewish origin were converted to the Christian faith, for there has been found an exceedingly curious epitaph, " written in Hebrew, Greek, and Latin," which doubtless marks the resting-place of a Christianized Jewess. The inscription in Greek letters reads HERE LIES FAUSTINA. At the foot is a very rough attempt to inscribe the Hebrew SHALOM, peace. The Jewish candlestick is in the centre the slab, on one side an oil-vessel, and on the other a palm-branch. The explanatión would seem to be, that a Jewess, upon conversion, took as her Christian name the Latin *Faustina,* and her friends at her death recorded upon her tomb her Hebrew origin, as well as her Christian faith.

In another instance, a female with a Jewish name, ELIASA, sets up a slab to the memory of a Roman husband, SORICIUS, inscribed

TO OUR GREAT GOD—ELIASA TO SORICIUS.

The centre of the slab exhibits the monogram of Christ, with the ends of the side branches turned up to form the figure of the candlestick, ingeniously combining, in a small compass, as in the former case, the idea of Jewish origin with Christian belief.*

The phonetic and trade symbols, and those which expressed faith in Christ, were not by any means the only symbolic figures made use of. In an ignorant age, it was needful to express in signs many things which in our times are conveyed without difficulty in writing.

* See Maitland's " Church in the Catacombs," pp. 76—78 and 210.

Thus *peace* and *hope* are symbolically depicted on the gravestones : peace by the dove and olive-branch; hope and security by the anchor; while the well-founded conviction of having entered into rest was well expressed by the ship in harbour.

Here are instances : a dove with an olive-branch in its mouth, and the word PAX, peace ; another dove with a branch in its claws, and the inscription—[**88**]

TO CENUARIA, A VIRGIN, WELL DESERVING; BURIED IN PEACE WITH GOOD WISHES.

Here is a dove with an anchor drawn on its breast, and the inscription—

IN CHRIST. DECEMBER, WHILE LIVING, MADE HIMSELF A BISOMUM.

Here is also a representation of an anchor, signifying the security of the Christian's hope ; a scriptural figure used in the Epistle to the Hebrews : " Which hope we have as an anchor of the soul, both sure and steadfast." *

The ship, also, of which you have here an illustration, refers likewise, in all probability, to a Scripture figure used by Peter ;† the reference being, it is supposed, to the prosperous entrance of a vessel into port. " For so an entrance shall be ministered unto you, abundantly, into the everlasting kingdom of our Lord and Saviour Jesus Christ."

There are many other significant symbols found, but I can do little more than name them. The crown and palm-branch are very frequent, referring evidently to the triumph and rewards of those who were " faithful unto death." These are also · Scripture emblems, repeatedly

* Heb. vi. 19.   † 2 Peter i. 11.

88

RELIGIOUS SYMBOLS.

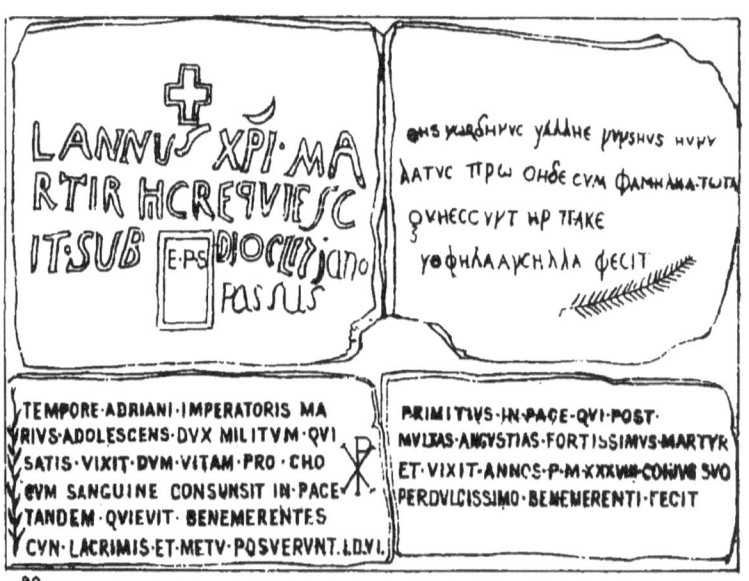

90

MARTYRS' EPITAPHS.

mentioned in the Book of Revelation. There is no reason
to conclude that these symbols marked particularly the
graves of martyrs; the reference is to the triumph of the
Christian over sin, the world, and the devil, rather than
over the weakness of the flesh in the hour of persecution.

Here is an illustration, in which the monogram of
Christ is surrounded by the palm-branches of triumph,
and surmounted by a crown, which shows to whose
strength the victory was attributed by these early Christians.

The inscription reads: [87]

FLAVIA JOVINA, WHO LIVED THREE YEARS AND THIRTY DAYS, A NEOPHYTE,
IN PEACE. DIED THE II BEFORE THE KALENDS.

In closing this account of the symbols used by these
illiterate Christians, I must guard myself against being
understood as approving of the use of symbolical representations of Divine things. A vast amount of idolatry,
both in Pagan and in professing Christian countries, can
be traced to the use of symbols, which are quite unnecessary now that education is so universal.

I now proceed to notice the subject of *martyrs' graves*.
The Christian will always take a deep interest in all that
concerns those who, at any period of the world's history,
have laid down their lives rather than surrender the faith
and hope of the Gospel, and deny the Lord who bought
them; but particular interest attaches to those who sus-
tained the brunt of the conflict with the powers of darkness in the infancy of Christianity. Unfortunately, ignorance and superstition have done much to render researches
into the subject distasteful to many, and difficult to all.
Every scratch on a gravestone has been construed into a

sign of martrydom, every symbol of trade into an imple-
ment of torture, and every bone found into a martyr's
remains. Such was the zeal and such the ignorance of
the professors of the Romish faith when the Catacombs
were re-opened, that a great part of the bones found were
carried away as precious relics, to sanctify, as it was
believed, the churches in which they were deposited. Of
Christians, therefore, whether martyrs or otherwise, very
few remains are to be found. Happily, the search for
bones was more zealously pursued than that for inscriptions ; and we can well spare the Romanists the bones, as
they have permitted us to draw "sermons in stones"
from the inscriptions which have been preserved, and
which, being printed, are now imperishable.

There is reason to believe that very few perfect inscriptions relating to martyrs now exist ; indeed, it does
not appear to have been the practice of the early Christians
to obtrude their own sufferings upon others; their inscriptions almost always point to a glorious immortality, and
seldom dwell upon present or past suffering. The idea
expressed by the Apostle* appears to have been ever
before them : "For our light affliction, which is but for a
moment, worketh for us a far more exceeding and eternal
weight of glory." "Peace" is inscribed on thousands of
graves ; "Suffering" on but very few. With the exception of a few fragments, on which the word "Martyr"
appears, and the case of ALEXANDER already alluded to
(page 76), there have been found in the Catacombs only
four well-attested instances of inscriptions alluding to
martyrdom.

Here are fac-similes of two and copies of two. Let

* See 2 Cor. iv. 8—18.

me speak of the copies first. One displays the palm-branch and monogram of the Saviour. The Emperor Adrian's name fixes the date at about the year A.D. 130 :

[90]—

IN THE TIME OF THE EMPEROR ADRIAN, MARIUS, A YOUNG MILITARY OFFICER, WHO HAD LIVED LONG ENOUGH, WHEN WITH BLOOD HE GAVE UP HIS LIFE FOR CHRIST. AT LENGTH HE RESTED IN PEACE. HE WELL-DESERVING SET UP THIS WITH TEARS AND IN FEAR, ON THE SIXTH BEFORE THE IDES OF ——. IN CHRIST.

This inscription was evidently erected in a time of actual persecution, "in tears and in fear."

Here is another inscription set up by a martyr's widow, telling, in few and touching words, of the suffer-ings of the flesh, and also of the pangs which must have racked the bosoms of those united in bonds of the tenderest affection. A class of suffering perhaps the most actually felt, but too much overlooked in our con-sideration of martyrs' trials in all ages.

PRIMITIUS IN PEACE. AFTER MANY TORMENTS, A MOST VALIANT MATRYR. HE LIVED THIRTY-EIGHT YEARS, MORE OR LESS. HIS WIFE RAISED THIS TO HER DEAREST HUSBAND, THE WELL-DESERVING.

Here, again, is a fac-simile of an inscription found by Boldetti; it is the sole known record in the Catacombs of the fearful Diocletian persecution. Its value is increased by the letters E P S, proving that the slab closed the actual resting-place of Lannus and his family. It reads:

LANNUS, CHRIST'S MARTYR, RESTS HERE. HE SUFFERED UNDER THE DIOCLETIAN PERSECUTION.
(E. P. S.) THE GRAVE IS FOR HIS POSTERITY.

The last inscription, of which I show you a fac-simile,

is of too much interest to be passed over without a more detailed notice.

It is written in an unusual Greek character, but the words are *Latin*.* It reads:

HERE LIES GORDIANUS, DEPUTY CF GAUL, WHO WAS EXECUTED FOR THE FAITH, WITH ALL HIS FAMILY. THEY REST IN PEACE. THEOPHILA A HANDMAID, SET UP THIS.

A palm-branch is added at the foot.

This epitaph, discovered by Aringhi in 1650, has caused much learned speculation. Why it should have been written in Greek characters unlike all others in the Catacombs, and why a maid-servant from Gaul (ancient France) should write in Greek at all, have been questions difficult to decide. It is thus satisfactorily explained by Dr. Maitland. †

" About thirty years after the time of Aringhi, Mabillon drew attention to an observation made by Julius Cæsar, ‡ that the Gallic Druids were accustomed to use Greek letters in their secular transactions, and that they had the management of the education of youth. This accounts for Theophila's Greek, some letters of which can scarcely be admitted within the pale of the standard alphabet. She afterwards learns Latin, but only by ear; this ill-assorted learning does not enable her both to write and speak any one language. Theophila has one resource, to express Latin words in Druidical Greek letters: in this way she contrives to record the martyrdom of her master.

" We are here met by a difficulty : we have made out,

---

* HIC GORDIANUS GALLIÆ NUNCIUS JUGULATUS PRO FIDE. CUM FAMILIA TOTA; QUIESCUNT IN PACE. THEOPHILA ANCILLA FECIT.

† "Church in the Catacombs," pp. 134—136.

‡ Cæsar, De Bello Gallico, lib. vi.

upon the strength of an obscure inscription, the story of
a Roman legate, a man high in office, martyred for the
faith. We have placed the incident in Rome, and fixed
upon the Catacombs as his burial-place. We have given
him a household, and, in particular, a faithful Christian
handmaid, who raises a monument to his memory. But
does history contain no notice of so remarkable an occurrence? Aringhi, who discovered the epitaph, knew of
none. About ninety years before Aringhi wrote, Surius
published a manuscript, entitled ' The Martyrdom of St.
Gordianus.' In this tract is described the conversion of
a Roman nobleman named Gordianus, through the preaching of Januarius the presbyter, who suffered in the time
of Julian; also, the baptism of Gordianus and his wife
Marina, together with a large part of his household,
amounting to fifty-three persons. Gordianus was martyred, and his body exposed before the temple of Minerva,
from which indignity it was soon rescued by one of the
household, who buried it in the Catacombs, in the Latin
Way. A coincidence more complete can scarcely be
desired."

The almost filial affection of this Christian maid-
servant for her martyred master reminds us strongly of
Mary of Bethany, her love for the Saviour and her fearless
avowal of her faith when she anointed Him in the house
of Simon the leper; * while the notoriety which has been
given to the loving and courageous act of Theophila the
handmaid reminds us also of the prediction of the Saviour
on that occasion : "Wheresoever this Gospel shall be
preached in the whole world, there shall also this, that
this woman hath done, be told for a memorial of her."

* Matt. xxvi. 6—13.

The Catacombs contain many representations of men and women standing with their hands outstretched; which figures were supposed by Roman Catholics to indicate the graves of martyrs. It is clear, however, that the assumption is unfounded, and that the position of the figures represents rather a sentiment than a fact; the standing with hands outstretched being the universal posture for *prayer* in the early Church at Rome.

I show you two representations, out of a great many which have been preserved [**91**]; one is that of a female, and the other represents the Apostle Paul. If you look also at the sarcophagus of Eutropus [**85**], before alluded to, and at Daniel in the Lion's den [**94**], you will perceive that both are represented in the same attitude.

This posture in prayer was common to both Pagans and Christians, as may be seen by reference to Virgil, a Pagan poet, as well as to Tertullian, a Christian writer. The latter, in his Apology, says: ·" For the emperors we supplicate the true, the living, the eternal God, in whose power they are : to whom they are second, after whom first. *With hands extended*, because harmless ; with heads uncovered, because not ashamed ; without a prompter, because from the heart we ask long life and every blessing for him. . . . . Then, while we *stand praying* before God, let the *ungulæ* tear us, the crosses bear our weight, let the flames envelope us, the sword divide our throats, the beasts spring upon us ; *the very posture of a praying Christian* (*i.e.*, erect, with hands outstretched like a cross) *is a preparation for every punishment.*"*

Christians in the Catacombs are universally repre-

* Tertullian, Apol., cap. 30.

PRAYING FIGURES.

LOVE-FEAST. FRESCO PAINTING.

sented as praying in this position, the practice of kneeling
in prayer having been introduced as a general practice at
a later date.* This fact affords valuable corroborative
evidence of the antiquity of the sculptures and works of
art found in the Catacombs; for, had fraud been attempted
to be practised, it would have displayed itself by inconsistencies similar to those which declare so unequivocally
certainly literary forgeries professing to be works of the
early Church.

Do not suppose that because I have pointed out to
you the primitive practice of the Church, as it regards
the posture for devotion, that I attach any weight to the
position of the body, or sympathise with those who treat
such matters as essentials of Christianity. It is lamentable
to reflect how often Christian has been estranged from
Christian, in consequence of a different practice as it regards the form in which a spiritual worship should be
rendered. Religion has long ceased to be a matter of
time, or place, or posture, as it was among Pagans; it is
now of the *heart* and not of the *knees, whether bent or*

---

* According to the authorities cited in the Rev. Lyman Cole-
man's "Antiquities of the Christian Church" (p. 100), the practice
of kneeling in public prayer was introduced as a penance, *kneeling*
being termed the less penance, in distinction from *prostration*, prescribed for greater offenders; standing in prayer was denied to
those who were under the Church's censure, it being esteemed
the prerogative and privilege only of consistent believers. It is
easy to trace the connection between the original practice of
causing *penitents* to kneel, and the feeling of *humility* so generally
connected with the kneeling posture in more modern times.
Kneeling in prayer was absolutely forbidden on the Lord's day
and on the Sabbath day, that is, the Saturday. See great variety
of authorities cited in that work, under chapter x., section 12,
notes 2—11.

unbent. Three thousand years have been insufficient to teach men the truth promulgated, even in the days of Samuel the prophet, that "the Lord seeth not as man seeth ; *for man looketh on the outward appearance, but the Lord looketh on the heart.*"*

The inscription, which is affixed to one of the slabs under consideration, reads—

BELLICIA, A MOST FAITHFUL VIRGIN WHO LIVED EIGHTEEN YEARS. IN PEACE. ON THE FOURTEENTH BEFORE THE KALENDS OF SEPTEMBER.

Bellicia is represented clothed in the dress then proper to unmarried females, the *stola instita,* or fringed cloak. In the other case, the only inscription is—

PAUL . PASTOR . APOSTLE .

Here the primitive simplicity of the early Church is observable ; no prefix of *Saint* had then been added to any of Christ's followers exclusively, but the term was applied, as in the Scriptures, to all alike who were sanctified by a true and living faith in Him.† Neither do we find any "nimbus," or "glory," or "aureole" surrounding the head of the Apostle, nor indeed the head of any Christians represented in the Catacombs. The practice, Pagan in its origin, had its commencement amongst Christians in the fifth century.‡ The simple

---

* 1 Sam. xvi. 7.

† See Rom. i. 7; 1 Cor. i. 2 ; 2 Cor. i. 1 ; Eph. i. 1; Phil. i. 1; Col. i. 2, etc., etc. There are fifty-seven instances in the New Testament, in which believers, as a class, are called "Saints," but no instance of the term applied to an individual to separate him from other believers.

‡ The earliest instance extant of the *nimbus, i.e.,* circle surrounding the head, as *used by Christians,* is found in a church at Ravenna, built in the fifth century; it is affixed to a figure of

and scriptural titles of "pastor" or shepherd, and "apostle," with a cross indicating union with Christ, were considered sufficient distinction for the great Apostle of the Gentiles, in a city in which some of his so-called apostolic successors have permitted to be attributed to them the titles and prerogatives which belong to God.

It is interesting to notice that, among other primitive practices of the early Church, the Catacombs afford illustration of the *agapæ*, or love-feasts. This practice is twice referred to in the New Testament : 2 Peter ii. 13, and Jude, 12th verse. It consisted of a social meal, generally connected with the reception of the Lord's Supper, in imitation of the example of our Lord and His disciples, who partook of the Passover Supper immediately before the institution of the Christian ordinance.* The love-feast usually formed part of the festival on the occasion of baptism or marriage, and was observed also at burials. In process of time, excesses were committed and abuses crept in, until the feasts were first banished from the Churches, and subsequently altogether abolished in Europe. † In the early ages of the Church, these meetings doubtless promoted Christian intercourse and brotherly love. Tertullian gives a particularly favourable

---

Christ.—See Twining's "Early and Mediæval Christian Art," plate 15, fig. 9, and plate 93, fig. 1.—Illustrations of it, *as used by Pagans,* may be seen in Pompeii, where it is affixed to the head of Circe and others.—Vide " Library of Entertaining Knowledge —Pompeii," vol. ii. pp. 92, 93, and amusing note as to its origin.

* Ignatius, Epist. ad Smyrn., c. 8.

† It is interesting to notice that the practice was found to exist among the Nestorian or Chaldean Christians of Central Asia, by Dr. Asahel Grant, and appears never to have been interrupted since apostolic times.—Vide Dr. Grant's "Nestorians," p. 57.

picture of them in his Apology.* He represents the meal as frugal and temperate; the conversation conducted under the conviction that God was present; prayer was offered, *the Scriptures read and explained*, and hymns sung; the kiss of peace and brotherhood, and a collection for those who were in want, accompanied the ceremony. It appears likely that the custom of celebrating wakes over dead bodies, as practised in Ireland and elsewhere, may be traced to this observance. The practice of holding feasts of charity has been of late years revived by some bodies of Christians, particularly by the Methodist Churches, and as "the cup which cheers but not inebriates" has been wisely substituted for the wine-cup, excess is avoided, and the practice is not exposed to the odium which once rested on it.

Here is an interesting painting, representing one of these feasts, found in a subterranean chapel in the cemetery of Marcellinus and Peter. [**92.**]

Three guests are seated at table; a young man supplies food from a table in the centre, while two matrons appear to preside; personifying, as the inscription would infer, " Peace" and " Love." On the table are seen a lamb, bread, and a cup, and a wine-flagon stands on the ground. Over the heads of the presidents are two contracted Latin inscriptions, which read PEACE, GIVE HOT WATER. LOVE, MIX FOR ME, referring to the almost universal custom in those days of drinking wine mixed with water.†

At the side of this painting are represented two cups, found elsewhere in the Catacombs, referring doubtless to the Lord's Supper; one of them contains cakes of bread.

---

* Apol., p. 93.   † Vide " Church in the Catacombs," p. 268.

I have now fulfilled my promise, by explaining to you that which is difficult and bringing before you that which is most interesting in relation to the inscriptions in the Catacombs; and now allow me, in conclusion, to say, *admire the wise providence of God* in His doings with regard to this subject.

He prepared beforehand a hiding-place for the Truth, a cradle for His persecuted church; or rather, I should say, He caused the Roman Emperors unwittingly to do so. Before Christianity arrived at Rome, the extensive quarries, which afterwards became the Catacombs, were excavated; but beyond this it is certain that some of the Roman Emperors condemned Christian soldiers to hard labour in digging sand and stone. This was the case in the reign of Maximian, and tradition states that the baths of Diocletian were built with material procured by the Christians.* This practice made these Christians acquainted with the intricacies of the galleries, and thus enabled them, in times of violent persecution, to become guides to those who resorted to these subterranean refuges, and facilitated that which must have been a dangerous and difficult task—the supply of the sufferers with food. We learn thus how God can make "the wrath of man to praise Him," "and the remainder of wrath" He can restrain. †

* "Church in the Catacombs," p. 34.   † Psalm lxxvi. 10.

LECTURE IV.

POPERY;

DEBASED, OR SPURIOUS CHRISTIANITY.

" I saw a woman sit upon a scarlet-coloured beast . . . .
having seven heads and ten horns . . . . The seven heads
are seven hills, on which the woman sitteth . . . . And the
woman which thou sawest is that GREAT CITY, which reigneth over
the kings of the earth."—REV. xvii. 3, 9, 18.

I NOW arrive at my concluding lecture, and apply myself
to answer an objection which has been made, and not
without some plausibility—"If Christianity is a Divine
remedy, why has it not effected more completely its
mission by removing evils which still afflict our world ?"
That it has accomplished enough to vindicate its
Divine character, I think will be conceded by most of you
who have listened attentively to my preceding statements.
That it might have effected more, I cannot deny ; that it
will accomplish more, I fully believe ; but I think that
you are entitled to an answer to the objection I have indicated, and shall proceed to supply one, so far as my
humble ability and limited time will permit.

Now, my answer to the objection is, simply—CHRIS-
TIANITY WAS CORRUPTED, AND IS, TO A GREAT EXTENT, COR-
RUPTED STILL.

To make use of a familiar figure, the Great Physician
left behind Him a *prescription* adequate to the remedy of

the evils of a sinful and wretched world. It gave evidence of its efficacy by its wondrous effects when first administered ; but it was tampered with : one ingredient was omitted here, another was added there, until it bore little resemblance to the original, which at last was put quite out of sight. Little wonder, then, that it ceased to cure !

The question arises, How do you prove this? I answer by bringing forward evidence as to the original treatment ; THE GRAVESTONES OF THE CATACOMBS WILL BE MY WITNESSES. They have furnished us with a contrast with Paganism ; they shall witness to the existence of a primitive, a pure, and an efficacious Christianity. As we call an aged man to prove, at law, a practice sanctioned by long usage, so we summon these silent witnesses, who will step forth from their hiding-places of from fifteen to eighteen centuries, and speak of the religion of Christ.

I am not about to speak of *men* but of a *system ;* I assert that a bastard, debased, spurious Christianity has usurped very extensively the place of the genuine faith. Not that I believe that there has ever been a time since · its introduction when true Christianity has not had some sincere and true professors, but rather, admitting that true Christians have, in different places and under different names, held fast their faith in Christ, and formed a Church, " whose names are recorded in heaven ;" yet I assert that a very wide-spread and general apostasy has prevailed throughout the length and breadth of professing Christendom, which has for many ages substituted a spurious for a genuine Christianity, even as it was clearly predicted in the passage placed at the head of this lecture and elsewhere in the sacred Scriptures.

Now, adhering to this figure, I ask, how would you

proceed to try a piece of doubtful coin which I might
tender to any of you in the way of business? You will
wisely submit it to such tests as you may possess. You
ring it : has it the sound which nature has given to silver ?
You place it between your teeth : is it soft or hard ? You
pass it through a gauge : do you find it of the standard
thickness ? You weigh it : is it due and lawful weight ?
If you still doubt, you can look it closely in the face :
does it really look what it professes to be ? If not, submit
it to a still closer scrutiny, assisted by such tests as the
chemist will supply, to detect the counterfeit, if it be one.

Now, in all this you would do wisely; and should we
not be equally, nay more, anxious to bring to the strictest
test all that which claims to be genuine Christianity, so
as to discover the spurious form, if it exist?

Now, we have the means at hand to test that which I
assert is debased Christianity. We can try it by HISTORY,
and inquire what have been the practices of its professors
—what its effects on the comfort, the happiness, the
morality of mankind. History tells a tale of oppression,
cruelty, persecution, avarice, and ambition, committed in
the name of Christ and His religion; of conversion at
the point of the sword; of confession extorted by the
rack; of slaughter and destruction carried on against
both infidels and Christians, in the name of Him who
" came not to destroy men's lives, but to save them."
The system of which I speak is charged by history with
these and many other grievous crimes ; that it has caused
and fomented war and bloodshed ; has deposed kings,
and absolved their subjects from their allegiance ; promoted treason and rebellion, effected revolutions to aug-
ment its power; that it has ever persecuted, when it was
strong enough to persecute with impunity and effect;

that it has invented more tortures, and exercised more ingenuity and refinement in cruelty, than any other system the world has heard of, not excepting ancient Paganism itself.

It is charged by history with falsehood the most un-blushing, frauds and forgeries the most indecent, impos-tures the vilest. It is charged by history, and stands convicted now before all eyes, as the great enemy to human liberty and progress. Liberty of speech it denies wherever it has the power. Liberty of inquiry it forbids ; take the cases of Copernicus and Galileo—one of whom was excommunicated, and the other died in the Inqui-sition, for pursuing scientific inquiry. Liberty of the subject to share in Government it has thwarted. Liberty of the press it has always shackled. Liberty of conscience it laughs to scorn. The most stupendous and brilliant works of human genius are closed and forbidden to those who submit to its thraldom. With true consistency, it has included in its list of prohibited books THE WORD OF GOD. Science, literature, a free press, free conscience, and the Bible being alike forbidden, the system of which I speak stands condemned by the voice of history, as a gigantic political conspiracy against the happiness, the purity, the liberty, and rights of mankind.*

As claiming to be from *God,* this system should be tried by *God's Word.* We can test it therefore by SCRIP-TURE—can weigh it in the balances of the Sanctuary. You have the balances in your own hands ; weighed in them, as it has been, again and again, it will be found grie-vously wanting. It is needless, however, to press this

---

* A concise outline of this subject will be found in a little work published by the Religious Tract Society, "The Testimony of History against the Church of Rome."

point, for the standard of comparison having been removed out of sight by those who would pass the spurious
article, they by this their own act of withholding the
Scriptures from their followers, admit that their system
cannot stand the test of God's Word.

Now, it is not my intention to undertake this analysis
either by the aid of *history* or of *the Bible*—time would
not permit my doing so with any advantage, and indeed
it has been done most effectually by others. But referring only to those tests incidentally, it is my purpose
rather to make use of the *inscriptions, sculptures, and
paintings* of the early Christians, in my reply to the
objection which we have in view.

And here you must allow me to remark that it is
exceedingly difficult to name and to define exactly this
system of which I speak ; just as it would be impossible
to denominate and classify all kinds of spurious coin in
circulation amongst us. It has assumed different forms
in different ages and countries, and does so still. It
corrupts the truth in proportion as it is furnished with
facilities for so doing by the darkness of ignorance around
it. It is by no means exclusively confined to one professing Christian Church, but, in different degrees, does
afflict, or may afflict, several organizations of professing
Christians. Its name is legion, but its principles are one.
But though *difficult to define* in all its workings, this
system can be traced home without difficulty to its source.
Just as disease of contagious or virulent character is
usually accompanied by sickness of a modified but kin-
dred type—the cholera, for instance, which sprang from
its bed in the Ganges, and spread around the world, with

its attendant maladies—so this evil system of which I speak can be traced to its origin, although its accumulated consequences can never be fully defined.

The chief guilt, "the head and front of this offending," *lies at the door of* PAPAL ROME.

In speaking henceforth of Popery, Rome, Romanism, or of Roman Catholicism, as it is absurdly called,* I must again state that I speak of a *system*, and not of *persons*. There may be, and doubtless are, many who are identified outwardly with this system who are not, in heart, of it; just as there may be, and doubtless are, those who do not profess to hold with this system, and yet, in spirit, their principles are one with it. I condemn the system, as I believe it contrary to Christ and His Gospel, and the greatest hindrance to the triumph of His religion on the earth; but I entertain no animosity towards the victims of the system. We may pity, and even love, the victim, while we denounce the system. We show no ill-will toward the slave when we denounce the evils of slavery; so I would be clearly understood as speaking with all Christian affection of those who are deluded by the falsehoods of Popery, while I use the words which truth compels towards the system itself.

It will be clear that, if I confine myself to the evidence furnished by the inscriptions, I shall not be able

---

* The word Catholic means *universal;* while Rome, and that which belongs to it, is *local.* Roman Catholic, therefore, is a contradiction in terms, being equivalent to "*universal local*"—an absurdity. There can be but *one universal* or *Catholic Church,* and that is confined to no nation, or kingdom, or people, or tongue: it is "the Church of the firstborn, whose names are recorded in heaven" (Heb. xii. 23); those who compose it are known there only with certainty.

to point out *every* error in the Romish system : a complete
body of divinity cannot be expected to be extracted from
gravestones. It is remarkable, indeed I may say provi-
dential, that in this case so much can be gathered from
such a source.

I will endeavour, so far as my limited time will permit,
to make plain to you how so great a corruption of the
truth as I have indicated came about.

The corruption of Christianity arose from various causes.

I need hardly say Christianity suffered from the in-
herent *corruption of the human heart;* but as it was
specially adapted to meet this evil and overcome it, we
must find some other cause which acted upon the instru-
mentality itself, and rendered it feeble in its operation.

Then : Christianity suffered from the persevering and
unceasing efforts of those who sought to *mingle with it
expiring Judaism.* Unable to comprehend the spiritual
character of Christ's religion, they strove to bring it
into subjection to the ceremonial law, which was intro-
ductory to it—*" the Schoolmaster "* dispensation, as Paul
terms it ; of this evil you can read for yourselves in the
Acts of the Apostles, and in almost all of Paul's Epistles.

Christianity likewise suffered from the *speculations,
the refined subtleties* of Greek and Roman philosophy.

Against all these sources of corruption the Scriptures
warned the early Church, as well as Christians of all
times. Again and again we find Paul expressing his
fears, his anxious solicitude on these points. " I fear,"
says he, " lest by any means, as the serpent beguiled
Eve through his subtlety, so your minds should be *corrupted from the* SIMPLICITY THAT IS IN CHRIST." Again :
" Beware lest any man spoil you through *philosophy* and

vain *deceit, after the traditions of men, after the rudiments of the world, and not after* CHRIST."*

Notwithstanding repeated warnings, the Church became corrupted from the simplicity of Christ's teaching, by reason of the influences I have just alluded to; but that corruption was as nothing compared with that which arose from another source, *the attempt to harmonize Christianity and Paganism.*

That no such attempt should be made while the two religions were in actual conflict is likely enough; but, when Constantine became favourable to Christianity, and both religions were tolerated, that which before was impossible now became practicable, and men were found who, from well-meant but mistaken motives, urged such a compromise as desirable.

Augustine thus writes : " When peace was made, the crowd of Gentiles (Pagans) who were anxious to embrace Christianity were deterred by this—that whereas they had been accustomed to pass the festivals in drunkenness and feasting before their idols, they could not easily consent to forego these most pernicious yet ancient pleasures. It seemed good, then, to our leaders to *favour this part of their weakness,* and for those festivals which they relinquish to substitute others in honour of the holy martyrs, which they might celebrate with similar luxury, though not with the same impiety."† A passage in Fos-

---

* All reference to the effects, for good or for evil, produced upon Christianity by its connection with the secular power is advisedly omitted; I entertain decided views on this point, but I conceive I shall most conduce to the usefulness of this little work by silence, on this occasion, upon a point so differently viewed by Christians.

† Augustine, Epist. 29.

broke's Encyclopædia informs us of the same fact, with more of detail. "The heathen were much delighted with the festivals of the gods, and unwilling to part with those delights; and therefore Gregory (Thaumaturgus), who died A.D. 265, and was Bishop of Neocæsarea, to facilitate their conversion, instituted annual festivals. Hence the festivities of Christians were substituted for the Bacchanalia and Saturnalia; the May games for the Floralia (games in honour of Flora); and the keeping of festivals to the Virgin Mary, John the Baptist, and divers Apostles, in the room of the solemnities at the entrance of the sun into the signs of the zodiac, according to the old Julian calendar." *

Of the truth, in the main, of these statements there can be no doubt, as evidences of the coincidence of Christian festivals with traces of Pagan practice remain to this day.†

I think I have said enough to satisfy you that there were causes enough at work to corrupt Christianity. I now proceed to the proof of the fact, from the evidence furnished by the Catacombs. In proceeding with the argument, my first object will be to satisfy you that the *Church of Rome does not now resemble the primitive Christian Church;* while, incidentally, I shall point out that the corruptions generally consisted in the introduction of

---

* Fosbroke's "Encyclopædia of Antiquities, Classical and Mediæval," vol. ii., pp. 571—591.

† For instance: The name of Easter, from the Saxon goddess "Eastor;" the ceremonies practised in Cumberland, Scotland, Ireland, etc., on St. John's Eve, which consist of offering cakes to the sun, and sometimes passing children through the smoke of a bonfire; the use of the Druid symbol, the misletoe, at Christmas, and of buns on Good Friday; and, in Roman Catholic countries, the Carnival, or modern Saturnalia, at Easter, etc., etc.

Pagan practices and ideas into the Christian system. The proof must often be of a *negative* character; no evidence being found of a practice, it may reasonably be assumed that it did not exist, provided it be such a practice as, under the circumstances, would have left traces of its existence.

And, first, with respect to the *ministry of the Gospel.* Various orders of men were, from the earliest ages of Christianity, set apart for ministering the Word of God and prayer, and for guiding, instructing, and edifying the Churches. These ministers of the Churches were of various orders, and were styled by different names. Respecting the standing, style, and office of these ministers in primitive times, much diversity of opinion exists among Christians, and much external division of the Churches unhappily arises from this cause. I am not about, then, to enter on this debatable ground, nor to raise questions upon points which, to my mind, appear to be of minor importance. The ordinary ministers of the early Church are termed, both in Scripture and elsewhere, bishops—otherwise overseers or superintendents; presbyters—otherwise elders, ministers, pastors; and deacons—otherwise church stewards or servants.*

Now, what I would have you notice is that, amongst all these terms applied to Christian ministers, there is no

* No reference is here made to the *extraordinary* ministrations of the Gospel in early times by apostles, prophets, or evangelists. In giving the *names* by which the ordinary ministers of the Gospel were called, I must be understood as being altogether silent upon the question of the *number* of distinct offices, and how far one *name* was used interchangeably for another.

reference at all to a *priesthood*. To my mind, the most influential corruptions of Christianity arose from the gradual introduction of the idea of a *mediatorial sacrificial officer*, similar to the priest of the Jewish or the Pagan economy. It is clear that no such institution can be traced to any teaching of our Lord, or of His inspired Apostles, who never, in the New Testament, speak of any priesthood in the Christian Church but in a sense which includes every true believer united to Christ—the last, the great, the " High Priest of our profession." *
Now, this is not an unimportant point, as it might, at first sight, appear; for if a priesthood (I speak of the office in the Pagan or Jewish sense) be granted, then a train of consequences follow—as, indeed, they have followed, to the grievous corruption of " the simplicity that was in Christ."

A *sacerdotal priesthood* being granted, an *altar* must follow, and usurp the place of a table in the Supper which Christ appointed; a *sacrifice* must accompany the *altar*, as it has done in the recent Church of Rome; and *sacerdotal and mediatorial officiators* at the altar must step between the believer and his great High Priest, who encouraged all to come unto the Father *through Himself*. In this way Christ, in the Romish Church, is dishonoured ; His office of Priest and Mediator is ignored ; His perfect sacrifice, offered " once for all," is continually re-offered, as it is alleged, in that Church ; His people are taught to confess to, and to rely upon, their fellow-sinners for forgiveness, while they possess the inestimable privilege of personal access to Himself.

* See all the passages in the New Testament, in which the words " priest " or " priesthood " are used in reference to Christianity, viz., 1 Peter ii. 5 ; ii. 9 ; Rev. i. 6 ; v. 10 ; xx. 6.

" For now one offering, ne'er to be renew'd,
    Hath made our peace for ever.   This now gives
Free access to the throne of heavenly grace.
No more base fear and dark disquietude :
He who was slain—the accepted victim—lives,
And intercedes before the Father's face."

In making these remarks upon what I consider to be
a great fundamental corruption in the Church of Rome,
I have no intention of reflecting upon the *name* of
"priest" assumed by ministers of certain of the Re-
formed Christian Churches, provided the *idea* be not im-
ported with the *name*.   Unhappily, for the elucidation of
this point, the poverty of the English language affords
us no term which answers to the sacerdotal office of the
Jews or Pagans ;* and the word *priest*, which is merely
a contraction of *presbyter*, an elder, is the only English
word we have to convey ideas altogether dissimilar.
Upon this point, rather than express my meaning in my
own words, I would quote those of one who dignified the
office to which I refer.†   "Deeply as Rome dishonours
Christ as the Prophet, she still more deeply dishonours
Him as the *Priest of His people*.   Take away the priestly
office of Christ, and the Gospel is the Gospel no more;
for nothing, therefore, should we be more jealous, than
for the sole, sovereign priesthood of Jesus.   This, Rome
miserably mangles.   She does so, in the first instance,
by perpetuating a pretended order of priests, to co-
operate with Christ in His priestly functions—an order,
in her view, just as essential to salvation, as is the great
High Priest of our profession.   I enter my protest most

* Ἱερεὺς in the Greek, and *Sacerdos* in the Latin.
† The Very Rev. Canon Stowell, M.A., Lecture, "Popery :
How it Dishonours Christ."

solemnly and deliberately against the idea that, under
the Gospel, there is any such character on earth as what
is properly called a *priest*. Human priesthood belonged
to a symbolical, material economy, which is passed; it
belonged to the letter, it does not belong to the spirit.
Priests, in the proper sense of the word, are no more;
they ceased when the true Priest came. It were happy
if, by our own beloved Church, the word 'priest' had
never been used, because it is liable to misconstruction;
though every candid scholar well knows that in her
Rubrics the word is never employed in its ancient meaning; it is but *presbyter* shortened to *prester*, and then,
for condensation's sake, to *priest*. That the Church
uses the word in no other sense must be evident to every
unbiassed mind; because she uses it *interchangeably with
the word minister*, clearly indicating that one term is used
as the equivalent of the other. In vain have the ingenuity and sophistry of those who, while their foot is
within our pale, have their hearts within the pale of
Rome, striven to torture the use of the word priest into
an indication that our branch of Christ's primitive Church
holds anything like the wretched figment of Rome, that
a sacrificing priesthood is still in existence. Rome has
transmuted the simple evangelist, the herald of grace,
the apostle or messenger, the pastor or shepherd, the
fisherman casting his net to catch souls, the steward of
the household that should give the servants their portion
of meat in due season—into a splendid sacrificing sacerdotal hierarchy. And, if you ask me, whence sprang
the monstrous structure of popish heresy and enormity?
I answer, from priestly ambition."

Upon this important point, which I trust I have
cleared from difficulty, what say the inscriptions in the

Catacombs at Rome ? *No such terms as answers to the sacerdotal officer of the Pagans or the Jews has been found.* The names used to designate Christian ministers are those I mentioned as being used in the Scriptures, viz., bishops, presbyters, pastors, deacons ; while *lectors, i.e.,* Scripture readers, *fossors, i.e.,* sextons, and *exorcists,* who took part in baptisms, have been also found as officers in the early Church.

Settle then, my friends, as you will, the particular form of Church government which you conceive to come nearest to the primitive type ; form each of you, as nearly as you can, correct ideas as to the offices, style, and functions of the various orders of the Christian ministry ; regard all faithful ministers of Christ as holding an office the most dignified and honourable, and "esteem them very highly for their work sake ;" but be careful not to derogate from the honour which belongs to the Lord Jesus Christ. Look to Him continually as your Great High Priest—man, to sympathize with your infirmity, and God, able and willing to pardon your sin. Regard Him as the great sacrifice offered for you, and look for no other. Behold Him as the great Mediator of the New Covenant, "who ever liveth to make intercession" for you. Value His ministers for their instruction and their guidance ; *but rely on Christ for the salvation of your souls.*

> " I other priests disclaim,
> And laws and offerings too :
> None but the bleeding Lamb
> The mighty work can do.
> He shall have *all the praise,* for He
> Hath loved, and lived, and died for me."

As the Church of Rome has altered the *character* of the

Christian ministers, so she has varied their *condition;* " for-
bidding to marry," as was predicted of a coming apostasy.* Thus a virtue was made of constrained celibacy.
Nothing of this kind had been introduced in apostolic
times. The New Testament tells us that Apostles and
Evangelists were married men,† while Paul expressly
asserts his liberty in this respect,‡ and enjoins that a
Christian minister should be the husband of one wife.§

The Catacombs declare unequivocally that the practice
of the Roman church is novel, and prove that all orders
of the clergy in primitive times were accustomed to marry.
Dr. Maitland has furnished us with examples of inscrip-
tions applicable to each order.||

Here are several, gathered from many, which prove
this point; and firstly, a *Bishop's* epitaph :—

MY WIFE, LAURENTIA, MADE ME THIS TOMB; SHE WAS EVER SUITED TO
MY DISPOSITION, VENERABLE AND FAITHFUL. AT LENGTH DISAPPOINTED
ENVY LIES CRUSHED: THE BISHOP LEO SURVIVED HIS 80TH YEAR.

Again : a *presbyter's* epitaph :—

THE PLACE OF BASIL THE PRESBYTER, AND HIS (WIFE) FELICITAS. THEY
MADE IT FOR THEMSELVES.

Again : the epitaph of a *presbyter's* daughter :—

ONCE THE HAPPY DAUGHTER OF THE PRESBYTER GABINUS. HERE LIES
SUSANNA, JOINED WITH HER FATHER, IN PEACE.

The epitaph of a *deacon's* wife I have already given
(p. 74). I need not here repeat it.

---

* 1 Tim. iv. 3.
† 1 Cor. ix. 5; Matt. viii. 14; 1 Pet. v. 13 ; Acts xxi. 9.
‡ 1 Cor. ix. 5.   § 1 Tim. iii. 2, 11, 12; 1 Titus i. 6.
|| Church in the Catacombs, pp. 247—251.

Here is reference to the wife of an *exorcist* :—

JANUARIUS THE EXORCIST MADE THIS FOR HIMSELF AND HIS WIFE.

Again : the epitaphs of a *lector* and a *fossor*, and their wives.

CLAUDIUS ATTICIANUS, A LECTOR, AND CLAUDIA FELICISSIMA, HIS WIFE.

TERENTIUS THE FOSSOR, FOR PRIMITIVA HIS WIFE, AND HIMSELF.

It will hardly be needful for me to tell you, after what has been said respecting a sacerdotal priesthood, that there can be no more *sacrifice* for sin in the Christian Church. The sacrifice of the mass had not then been invented, nor indeed was it thought of until the ninth century, that is, some four hundred years after the Cata-combs were closed. You will be quite prepared to hear that no trace of any such sacrifice can be found in them. And so with respect to an *altar* in this sense. A Chris-tian poet, Prudentius,* who wrote in the fourth century, speaks of the *table* (*mensa*) on which the sacramental elements of bread and wine were placed in the Catacomb chapels, and he only uses the word altar (*ara*) when he is referring to prayer and praise, which is spoken of in Scripture under the figure of a spiritual sacrifice.†

How the *table* became the slab which closed the grave of a martyr, how the *tombstone* became elevated into an *altar*, and how in course of time the simple commemo-rative *supper* became a *sacrifice*—a meal became a mass, it would be unprofitable to narrate in detail. Such changes, however, took place, and such continues to be the corrupt practice of the Church of Rome. The Re-formed Churches, however, have retraced their steps,

---

* " Church in the Catacombs," p. 342.   † Heb. xiii. 15.

and follow the scriptural and primitive practice of observing the Supper as instituted by their Lord; have discarded the unmeaning and inappropriate *altar*, and have reinstated the primitive *table*.

Am I not justified in affirming that, in all these respects, a great departure has taken place " from the simplicity which was in Christ," and that the Church of Rome presents us with a corrupted, paganized form of Christianity ?

I now pass to another point. Rome not only dishonoured Christ as it regarded His office of Priest, but by degrees she exalted one human being after another, to share in the dignity of His office as *Mediator*. Apostles, martyrs, the Virgin Mary, disembodied spirits of men and women, also angels, she clothed with the omnipresent attributes of God, and taught that they should be addressed in prayer as intercessory mediators. This corruption of Christianity, the introduction of *demon* or spirit-worship, can also be *directly* traced to a Pagan origin—the regard shown, and worship often rendered to the *Divine Manes*, or disembodied spirits of great men, supposed to be deified under that system.

That such an error should have crept in very early in the history of Christianity is not to be wondered at, when we consider how the primitive Christians were circumstanced ; retaining naturally some of the traditional ideas of Paganism, and associated as they were in the Catacombs with the remains of those they loved and honoured in life.

On the gravestones of their hiding-places we read the history and discern the first buddings of this corruption, but it did not reach its height until long

after the Catacombs were closed as Christian cemeteries.* First came a pious *sentiment* breathed in prayer
over the grave, and rudely scratched upon the stone by
the hand of a loving and mourning friend—such as —

SWEET FAUSTINA MAY YOU LIVE IN GOD.

ZOTICUS, BE OF GOOD CHEER.

BOLOSA, MAY GOD REFRESH THEE.

Then, having thus accustomed themselves to address
the dead, came the next step in the declension — the
expression of hope that the departed, being in Christ,
might use his influence on behalf of those left behind in
the flesh.

The only inscription of this character in the Lapidarian Gallery reads :—

GENTIANUS, A BELIEVER, IN PEACE, WHO LIVED XXI YEARS, VIII MONTHS,
AND XVI DAYS. ALSO IN YOUR PRAYERS PRAY FOR US FOR WE KNOW
THAT YOU ARE IN CHRIST.

Then came actual praying at the grave of the departed, and seeking an interest in his intercessory
prayers, which evidently began to be practised before
the end of the *fifth* century ; then followed, naturally
enough, when the light of the glorious Gospel came to
be hid, the removal of the bones of the deceased to sanc-

* "In the Lapidarian Gallery (if it be not rash to pronounce
summarily upon the contents of so vast a collection), the name of
the Virgin Mary *does not once occur.* Nor is it to be found *once* in
any truly ancient inscription contained in the works of Aringhi,
Boldetti, or Bottari. Should any exception be discovered, it will
not weaken the astonishing contrast existing between the ancient
and mediæval churches in this particular."—" Church in the
Catacombs," p. 333.

tify some church, and to render efficacious the prayers offered near them; last of all came the worship of the *image*, or *picture* of the deceased, and the idolatry of the degraded and ignorant Pagan was revived in all but the name. Well says Dr. Maitland, " the Pantheon at Rome, originally devoted to *Jupiter and all the gods,* was dedicated to the *Virgin Mary and all the saints* : the building seemed to be Christianized, but in truth it was Christianity that was Paganized. Provided *men* are worshipped there, it matters little by what names they are invoked."*

My friends, so easy is it to descend when we have once entered upon a downward course. Let us cling more closely than we have ever yet done to spiritual worship, never forgetting the promise of the Great Mediator to those who believe on Him : " Whatsoever ye shall ask the Father *in my name* He will do it for you ;" and that it is declared in inspired Scripture that *" He ever liveth to make intercession for us."*

But I have not yet done with *saint worship;* in " the lowest depth " which we have explored, there is even " a deeper still." The Church of Rome having abandoned the guidance of the Holy Scriptures, forsaken " the guide of her youth," and forgotten " the covenant of her God," she appears to have been left to fall into error so palpable and obvious, that it might act as a warning to deter Christ's true followers from being allured by her blandishments or deceived by her lofty pretensions.

From the worship of the disembodied *spirits,* the *mortal remains,* and then the *representations* of saints, she fell into the absurdity of setting up imaginary mediators, who *never had any real existence at all.* The statements

* " Church in the Catacombs," p. 301.

which I 'shall bring before you would, under other and less serious considerations, provoke laughter; but they might well draw tears on behalf of ignorant and fallen human nature; they are derived all of them from Roman Catholic writers.

The origin of this error also can be traced to the remains found in the Catacombs of Rome.

Mabillon, speaking of these remains, says, " There are dug up two sorts of bodies, the one with neither name nor inscription, the other with one or both. Saints of the first kind *have names given them by the Cardinal Vicar, or by the Bishop,* who presides over the Pontifical Chapel. Saints of this description are said to be baptized." *

But poor human bones were not only made into *saints,* and *named,* but they were many of them elevated into *martyrs* as well. A " Holy Congregation of Relics," held in the year 1668, issued a decree : "The Holy Congregation having carefully examined the matter, decides that the palm and vessel (cup) tinged with blood are to be considered *most certain signs of martyrdom.* The investigation of other symbols is deferred for the present." †

While antiquarians are at issue as to the substance found staining certain cups placed in the graves, being divided in opinion between *wine, blood,* and *fragrant spices,* " the Holy Congregation" steps in and settles the matter, by raising the owners of the graves to the crown of martyrdom; it exhibits unlooked-for moderation and wisdom in postponing " for the present " the consideration of the other symbols.

Raoul Rochette tells us of one of these manufactured

* Mabillon's Posthumous Works, vol. ii. pp. 251, 287.
† " Church in the Catacombs," p. 174.

martyrs, and, although a Romanist, expresses grave doubts as to the genuine character of the article. This new saint, adopted so recently as 1803, was transported from Rome to Perugia; on his gravestone was repre- sented a pair of forceps, and the words—

D. M. S. (Sacred to the Divine *Manes*—a Pagan formula).

BERNERUS LIVED XXIII YEARS AND VII MONTHS.

On this inscription M. Rochette remarks, "In the absence of any *certain signs of Christianity*, this instru- ment may be considered as belonging to his profession. Bernerus therefore may have been a poor *blacksmith, Christian if you will, or Pagan,* which supposition accords better with the character of his epitaph, excepting for the vessel of blood (?) found in his grave, which is con- sidered an indubitable sign of Christian sanctity." *

Poor Bernerus—or more probably Venerius—was doubtless a Pagan blacksmith, and is now " indubitably" a martyr in glory—let us charitably hope that he is so ; at all events, let us learn to be careful how, with our fallible judgments and ignorance of men's hearts, we follow such examples, and exercise God's prerogative of separating and distinguishing saints from sinners, other- wise than by God's test; † and let all Christians be thankful that their acceptance or rejection will not de- pend upon guessing antiquarians, or even a " Council of Relics," but rather that it is surely written, " THE LORD *knoweth them that are His.*" ‡

Two more instances of blundering in this unholy work

* Mémoires de l'Academie des Belles Lettres et d'Inscriptions, tom. xiii., cited in " Church in the Catacombs," p. 181.

† " By their *fruits* ye shall know them," Matt. vii. 16, 20.

‡ 2 Tim. ii. 19.

of making mediators are mentioned by Mabillon, and quoted by Dr. Maitland.* One blunder, you will perceive, arose from ignorance of the Latin grammar, and the other from a defective knowledge of Roman antiquities.

An inscription was found in the Catacombs:

D. M. (To the Divine *Manes*—a Pagan formula)

JULIA EUODIA THE DAUGHTER MADE THIS TO HER CHASTE AND WELL-DESERVING MOTHER, WHO LIVED LXX YEARS.

Never was a saint more carelessly manufactured; not knowing, or not heeding, the difference between the nominative and dative cases, the finder of the inscription concluded that the grave contained the remains of *Julia Euodia*, and established Saint Julia Euodia accordingly. This occurred at Tolosa; but the light of the Latin grammar subsequently dispelled the illusion, and deprived Julia of her saintship, by showing that it was not her tomb, but that of her *" chaste and well-deserving mother."*

The other case was equally unfortunate. An ancient fragment of stone having been found inscribed thus, S. VIAR, it was taken to be the epitaph of a Saint Viar, and certain well-meaning persons, says Dr. Maitland, "nothing daunted by the singularity of the name, or the total want of evidence in support of his sanctity, boldly established his worship." Having subsequently applied to Pope Urban for indulgences (that is, remission of punishment for sin on account of prayers addressed to the saint), the antiquarians, those troublesome people,

* " Church in the Catacombs," pp. 182, 183.

so difficult to satisfy without full inquiry, sent for the stone, when it was immediately found to be a fragment with part of the title of Surveyor of the Highways; the S being the last letter in *Præfectus*,* and the VIAR being the four first letters of *Viarum;* it formed, doubtless, part of a milestone.†

Another instance must be quoted, because it shows a boldness of invention which throws these individual instances into the shade. If any of you have been to Cologne, on the Rhine, or have read of that "holy city," you will know that it is unrivalled for the number and sanctity of the remains of saints, apostles, and prophets which it possesses—"a huge museum of mouldering anatomy, useless alike to the living and the dead, and only commemorative of the weakness, darkness, igno-rance, and superstition of the human mind;" thus writes a recent traveller, Dr. James Johnson. The Doctor is incorrect, however, in saying that the remains are "use-less alike to the living and the dead;" the *dead* are, doubtless, beyond the reach of their influence, but the *living* reap a fine harvest ·from the gifts of the super-stitious; and the payments made, I am ashamed to say, by curious Protestants, who constantly visit this bone-house, are sufficient to keep swarms of priests and monks in idleness and luxury, and to perpetuate, if continued, fraud and superstition to the end of time. The Doctor

---

* Or the genitive or plural of *Curator Viarum*, an office fre-quently referred to in the Catacomb inscriptions.—See " Aringhi, Roma Subterinea," vol. ii., pp. 338, 339, etc.

† The lecturer, to make this plain to an uninformed audience, should copy the inscription thus, as a diagram: *Præfectu*S VIAR*um*, or *Curatori*S VIAR*um*. The same remark applies to the inscrip-tion next referred to.

himself admits that he was "silly enough to spend some days and dollars in exploring these mummeries;" indeed, keeping a bone-shop is the best business going in that holy city. It would be quite impossible for me to enumerate all the wonders of this kind that it contains; suffice it to say, that there is some of the *milk of the Virgin Mary*, the head of the Apostle Peter, "*les entrailles*" of Queen Mary de Medicis, and the skulls of the three wise men who offered gifts and adoration to the infant Saviour. I need not say that the *brains* of the *wise men* are *not* at Cologne, but the skulls are as empty as the heads of those who pay for a sight of them.

But all these relics are inconsiderable, compared with the vast collection in the Church of St. Ursula; here repose the mortal remains of a vast "army of martyrs;" no less than the bones of *eleven thousand English virgins*. How they came there is somewhat uncertain, and statements respecting their history are very contradictory. It is reported that they were on their voyage to Rouen, and either took the veil, or sacrificed their lives, to avoid marriage with the barbarous Huns, who then possessed the city. What eleven thousand young, unmarried ladies had to do at Rouen at all, or why, in such times, or indeed at any time, they forsook the shelter of the maternal roof, and in what fleet they crossed the sea, are points upon which history does not inform us. There are the bones, however; the Church of Rome has determined their sanctity, and instituted a service to their honour.*

* The Salisbury Breviary of 1555 (that is, service-book of that diocese previous to the Reformation) gives the following prayer for the feast of the eleven thousand virgins: "O God, who, by the glorious passion of the blessed virgin, thy martyrs, hast made

All this history of the eleven thousand virgin saints and martyrs is, doubtless, to be traced to the same origin as the other instances which have been brought forward —an incorrect rendering of an obscure inscription.

"There is nothing," says Dr. Maitland, "to contravene the supposition that the whole story is founded upon a mistaken rendering of the inscription—URSULA . ET . XI . MM . VV—interpreted '*Ursula and eleven thousand virgins,*' instead of '*Ursula and eleven virgin martyrs.*' " * Indeed, in a list of relics, published in the year 1117, some of "the remains of the *eleven* virgins" are mentioned; these bones had not then increased, as they did afterwards, a thousand-fold.

I am fearful that I have wearied you with the recital of these instances of saint-manufacture, and conclude this part of the subject by informing you, very briefly, of a well-known *invention* of a saint, still worshipped by the Church of Rome, notwithstanding the forgery has been rendered apparent, and has been exposed by learned men of that faith. I refer to the case of St. Veronica, whose name and existence are derived from the words *Vera icon* (a true likeness), formerly inscribed under pictures which purported to be representations of Christ. These certified copies came in time to be called *Veronicæ*, and were known by that name to Christian writers. It was not until the fourteenth century that Rome con-

---

this day a holy solemnity to us, hear the prayers of thy family; and grant that we may be freed by the *merits and intercessions of those* whose feast we this day celebrate," etc. ("Church in the Catacombs," p. 163). Nothing could more clearly prove that the Church of Rome makes *intercessory mediators* of saints than this passage.

* "Church in the Catacombs," p. 163.

structed out of legends, based upon the ignorant use of
the word Veronicæ, the saintship and history of Saint
Veronica, and established her worship. There is a
colossal statue of this supposed saint in St. Peter's, at
Rome; a prayer, issued by Pope John XXII., in which
the representation of Christ is addressed, obtains for those
who use it ten thousand days' indulgence. "The hand-
kerchief of Saint Veronica is publicly worshipped in
Rome on stated occasions, and the ceremony is performed
with the utmost splendour; no part of the Romish ritual
is more calculated to strike the imagination." *

Alas! "how has the faithful city become an harlot!"
In place of the worship of her Lord and Saviour, we
find the Church, whose "faith was spoken of throughout
the world," † and whose early professors joyfully went
to the flames, the beasts, or the torture, rather than com-
mit the remotest act of idolatry, now glorying in her
shame, tendering homage and worship to departed saints,
disembodied spirits, and disentombed remains of mor-
tality, even imaginary men and women, who exist only
in the lying legends she has invented.

Said I not truly that the religion which Rome presents to her votaries is a *debased, paganized, spurious*
form of Christianity?

I have spoken of the dishonour done to Christ by
the Church of Rome, as it regards his office of Priest
and Mediator. I have also hinted at the dishonour done
to the sacrifice which He offered of Himself, by the institution of a perpetually-recurring sacrifice, that of the
mass. I now come to speak of dishonour done to Him

---

* "Church in the Catacombs," pp. 160, 161.   † Rom. i. 8.

by another doctrine introduced by the Church of Rome, that which teaches that there is a *purgatory*, in which Christians, after death, are cleansed or purged from the *temporal* punishment due to them. I need not pause to convince you that in Scripture there is no foundation for such doctrine. Complete, immediate pardon and salvation are there offered to all true believers in Jesus Christ, without any reservation; not on account of their merits, but by virtue of the perfect sacrifice which Christ offered for them. We are assured that "the blood of Jesus Christ cleanseth from *all* sin;"* the sacrifice was complete—"a full, perfect, and sufficient sacrifice, oblation, and satisfaction for the sins of the whole world." †

Now Rome asserts the *insufficiency* of that sacrifice, and tells us, that what the Saviour could not do, and did not do, her priests have power to accomplish, that is to release suffering souls from punishment. This is a serious subject, and not to be spoken of lightly. The Bible speaks of two states or conditions after death : one of everlasting destruction from the presence of God, and the other of eternal and unalloyed happiness. No intermediate state, such as the Romish purgatory, is ever referred to. Those who are blessed enough to attain to heaven are assured that its blessedness is immediate and complete. "Absent from the body, present with the Lord," is the Scripture doctrine. ‡

No such comforting doctrine to pardoned sinners is held out by the corrupt system of which I speak. To the believer Rome can only promise that, when "absent from the body," the soul descends, for a period more or less

* 1 John i. 7.
† Communion Service of the Church of England.
‡ 2 Cor. v. 8.

protracted, into purgatorial flames, there to make up in
punishment that which was deficient in the atonement
made by Christ. This false doctrine places in the hands
of the priest a power such as no earthly potentate
possesses ; over the ignorant and superstitious he wields
the " powers of the world to come;" he assumes the prerogative of Christ, who "openeth and no man shutteth,
and shutteth and no man openeth."* In fact, this
doctrine places in the hands of the priest the key of the
prison-house, and he has not been loath to use it as the
key to this world's treasure. To teach that there was a
purgatory, that the duration of the detention there is uncertain, that it can be shortened or prolonged at the will
of the priesthood, is the most daring assumption of power,
and, at the same time, the most profitable scheme of priest-
craft, which the world has witnessed.

But you will ask me as to the extent or duration of
this assumed punishment due to Christians. I can only
answer the question by informing you of the amount of
remission of this punishment, which diverse Popes have
awarded, by way of indulgence, on certain prescribed
terms. This will give you some idea of the probable
extent of this purgatorial process, and of the comfort
which Christians dying in that Church must enjoy in the
prospect of death.†

Pope John XXII. granted on one occasion 300 days
of pardon ; Pope Boniface to all who " say a lamentable
contemplation for our blessed Lady," etc., seven years
and forty Lents of pardon. John XXII., on another

---

* Rev. iii. 7.

† I gather these instances of indulgence or remission of punishment from the "Collection of Records," in Part II. of Bishop
Burnet's " History of the Reformation," pp. 38—58.

occasion, offered 3000 days of pardon. Another indulgence granted by five holy fathers, Popes of Rome, con-confers 500 years and so many Lents of pardon. Pope Boniface VI. was more indulgent still, and granted, for the repetition of certain prayers called *Agnus Dei*, 10,000 years of pardon. Pope Sixtus, in consideration of a prayer to be devoutly repeated before the image of the Virgin, granted 11,000 years of pardon. Burnet mentions another case, in which there was granted "to all them that before this image of pity devoutedly say five *Paternosters*, five *Ave-Marias*, and a *Credo*, piteously beholding those arms of Christ's passion, 32,755 years of pardon ; and Sixtus the Fourth, Pope of Rome, hath made the fourth and fifth prayer, and hath doubled his foresaid pardon;" that is, he extended his forgiving power to 65,510 years. What, let me ask, comes of the forgiveness of *all* sin by the blood-shedding of Christ, if there can remain to believers (Christians, mark you), *sixty-five thousand years of purgatorial punishment?*

I need hardly point out to you that this doctrine re-introduces that which Christ condemned and denounced —the *sale of pardon*, for pardons and indulgences are *sold* in the Church of Rome to those who can pay for them.* Among Pagans, the rich could procure that which the poor could not; but the Gospel of the Saviour was to be communicated to the poorest " without money and without price ;" and, when John the Baptist sent from his prison to inquire as to the truth of the Messiah's claims, Christ pointed, as evidence, to the novel fact that "the *poor* have the Gospel preached to them." The religion of Jesus Christ, in its pure form, is a religion

* See a little work entitled "The Religion of Money," by N. Roussel. Seeleys and Co.

especially for the *poor man;* and you may be certain that is spurious religion which exacts a toll as the condition of entering heaven. The most costly sacrifice which could be offered has been slain for you, and if you offered all the gold which the world contains, it would be but dross, and valueless, compared with the *unsearchable riches of Christ.* Obtain an interest in that offering; "hold fast the profession of your faith without wavering;" and you may laugh to scorn all the idle and crafty tales of a purchasable exemption from purgatory.

Before I state what the Catacombs tell us of purgatory, allow me to inform you that this Romish doctrine does not even possess the merit of originality; it is a clumsy but crafty imitation of a *Pagan* idea, which is as clearly written in the Æneid of the Pagan Virgil, as if that poet had been a Roman Catholic. He thus writes :—

> "Nor death itself can wholly wash their stains;
> But long-contracted filth e'en in the soul remains.
> The relics of invet'rate vice they wear;
> And spots of sin obscene in every face appear.
> For this are various *penances* enjoined;
> And some are hung to bleach upon the wind;
> Some plung'd in waters, others *purg'd* in fires,
> Till all the dregs are drain'd, and all the rust expires.
> Then are they happy, when by length of time
> The scurf is worn away of each committed crime;
> No speck is left of their habitual stains,
> But the pure ether of the soul remains." *

And now for the witness of the Catacombs. Of all the doctrines of which I have to speak, none would so certainly have been referred to on gravestones as the doc-

* "Æneid," Dryden's Version, Book vi, pp. 998—1011; see Original, Book vi., pp. 736—747.

trine of purgatory, if any such ideas had then been entertained by the early Christian Church. What expres-
sions of desire for the prayers and alms of the living to
extricate souls from the flames would have been inscribed!
Now what is the fact? *No mention whatever, not even the
most incidental reference to the state of purgatory, has been
found in the Catacombs.* IN GOD. IN CHRIST. IN PEACE.
IN REFRESHMENT. IN THE HOME OF THE ETERNAL GOD.
BORNE AWAY BY ANGELS. RESTING. SLEEPING. IT IS
FORBIDDEN TO WEEP. HE LIVES ABOVE THE STARS.
Such are the invariable echoes of the galleries of the
Catacombs. *" No condemnation to them who are in Christ
Jesus." "Absent from the body, present with the Lord."
"Having a desire to depart and be with Christ."* Such
were the doctrines and the faith of the early Christians.
They believed in the gracious words once spoken to a
poor, wretched sinner, snatched from a sinful world and
ignominious death, to grace the Saviour's triumphant
entry into the world of spirits, there to show Himself a
Redeemer, *" mighty to save "*—*"* THIS DAY *shall thou be
with Me in Paradise."*
    Again, I ask, am I not justified in saying that a cor-
rupt, a debased, a spurious, a Paganized Christianity has
been introduced? That each of the corruptions to which
I have referred—the sacerdotal priesthood, the sacrifices,
the mediators many, the doctrine of purgatory—are to
be attributed mainly to the reintroduction of Paganism,
to the dishonour of primitive and vital Christianity?

    You were told, in the outset of this lecture, that of
which you were doubtless well aware—that Rome practi-
cally *shuts up the Holy Scriptures* to her followers. It is
needless to detain you by attempting to prove that which

I am convinced you all believe—that the Scriptures contain commands and encouragements to read, to search,
and to understand what is contained in them, according
to the ability which God shall confer upon each one of us.
Now, that which we believe and·practise on this
point was the belief and practice of the early Church.
The Bereans were commended for searching the Scriptures.* Timothy was congratulated that he had known
them *from childhood*, and enjoined to give attention to
reading them.† But we are not confined to Scripture
for proof of this fact. I have already quoted the words
of Tertullian (p..112), who lived in the second century:
he informs us that at love-feasts *"the Scriptures were
read and explained."* Also, Justin Martyr says, "Upon
the day called Sun-day,‡ all that live either in city or
country meet together at the same place, where the *writings of the apostles and prophets are read*, as much as the
time will give leave." §

The fact, also, of the office of *lector* (reader) existing
proves that the public service of religion consisted largely
of Scripture-reading. But the fact is so notorious that
the Scriptures formed the chief study. of the early Christians, that it must be quite unnecessary for me to say
more, except it be that every Christian writer of the first

* Acts xxvii. 11.   † 2 Tim. iii. 15, 16; :v. 13.
‡ The apologist is addressing Pagans, and therefore uses the
Pagan term "*Sun-day*" (*Dies Solis*). It were well that this term
were less used amongst us, and that the primitive term, and that
used in the Scriptures and *found in the Catacombs*, were substituted for it, viz., "THE LORD'S DAY" (*Dies Domini*). In times in
which the Divine origin of the institution, and the perpetual
obligation of its observance, are brought into question, the
change would neither be unmeaning nor without its effects.
§ Justin Martyr's " First Apology."

three centuries quotes largely from the Scriptures, which he must have possessed; indeed, it has been asserted with much truth, that if the sacred writings had been lost or destroyed, nearly the whole could have been recovered from the Christian writings of the first three centuries.

But you will inquire—What say the Catacombs on this point? The evidence is as abundant and satisfactory as could be desired. The galleries of the Catacombs afford us *pictorial illustration* of the fact. Christian artists of the Catacombs drew upon Scripture history for their inspiration; it was the only history they were acquainted with or cared to know.

Were we altogether in ignorance of the early developments of Christian art at Rome, there would be four things which we should picture to ourselves as probabilities in relation thereto :—

Firstly. Considering the abundance of suitable material, the perfection to which the fine arts had attained, and the national aptitude of the Romans for sculpture, we should expect to find traces of art left, even by the humble Christians of the Catacombs.

Secondly. We should expect to find that their *religion* formed very much the theme upon which they exercised their artistic genius.

Thirdly. Amidst persecution, suffering, and uncertainty of life, we should expect that they would select such subjects as would depict them own position, or shadow it forth by the parallel suffering or triumphs of others.

Fourthly. Reflecting that they were many of them Pagans by education, we should be prepared to expect some blending of ideas, Pagan and Christian, in the designing of their works of art.

Now it is interesting to discover that in all these respects the fine arts, as developed in the Catacombs, answer exactly to the conditions which we should have predicted concerning them. Much artistic merit in treatment and execution is often apparent; Scripture history is almost invariably the subject of illustration. The sufferings of God's people, or their deliverances from death, are the predominant topics (with matchless delicacy of feeling *their own are never obtruded*) : while Pagan inconsistencies occasionally peep out, affording gratifying *criteria* of the genuine character of the works discovered.

I now proceed to review some few of these interesting works of art, remarking very briefly upon each in passing, and, first, of the Old Testament subjects.

Noah, delivered in the ark, the type of those who had sought refuge in the Christian Church, was not likely to be forgotten. He is very often represented, generally in the act of receiving the dove with the olive-branch, signifying peace, hope, and reconciliation. Here is one representation of him [**93**], which may be taken as a specimen of a very numerous class. The ark is reduced to a mere chest, and the patriarch is alone. The artist's type is evidently derived from a Pagan coin then in existence,* and as it was his intention to convey an idea or sentiment, and not to produce an historical painting, it was more easily accomplished by representing Noah and the bird only, than by surrounding him with his family and the representatives of the animal world.

Next to Noah, perhaps Jonah is the general favourite. His history was considered typical of death and the resurrection. "In subterranean chapels," says Dr. Maitland, "when the living were separated from the dead by

* The Apamean medal.

a mere tile or slab of stone, and sometimes liable to be
mingled with them by the violence of their enemies, even
before the conclusion of their worship, the hope of a future
life naturally occupied a prominent place in their creed
* * * and all that could help a trembling faith to
seize the joyful reality was eagerly adopted. Jonah
escaping from the whale, or reclining beneath the gourd,
may be everywhere seen; at first scratched on the walls,
and afterwards sculptured on the sarcophagi. In the
emblem of a risen saint, the sins and sorrows of the
original hero were forgotten. * * * But there is yet
further meaning in this oft-repeated sculpture : ' a greater
than Jonah is here.' It was the Divine application of
this figure to the death and resurrection of Christ that
gave to it peculiar interest; for, by a happy inference,
the Church saw, in the rising of her Head, the certain
resuscitation of his members. In this small fragment.
of marble the Christian of ancient times traced
his own career; his passage from the unstable ele-
ment too well expressing his present life through the
gate of death, not inaptly represented by the terrible
monster, suffered to engorge though not to retain his
prey."*

Here [93] are two representations of Jonah, one of
them combined with that of Noah just referred to ; they
are both of them sculptured on sarcophagi. The upper
drawing represents his ejection from the ship into the
mouth of the great fish, and his subsequent escape from
the sea monster. The lower sculpture shows his escape
from the jaws of the fish to repose peacefully, which is
well told, beneath the overhanging gourd. The whole is
evidently symbolical, emblematical, and not strictly his-

* "Church in the Catacombs," pp. 303—305.

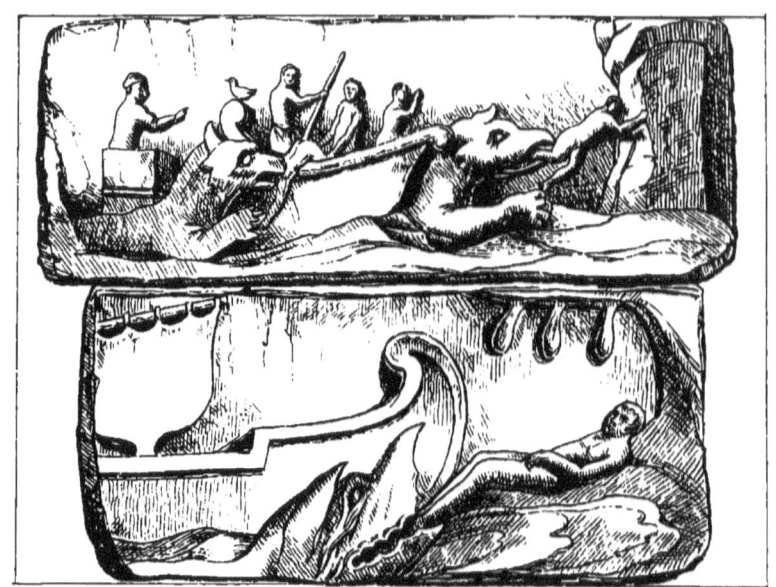

93

NOAH, AND JONAH.

94

DANIEL & THE LIONS. FRESCO PAINTING.

torical. The very *rock* to which Jonah clings has probably reference to the common Scripture emblem for
Christ.

Here are other Old Testament subjects, all of which
will bear a similar explanation. Daniel delivered from
the lions, a fresco painting [94] ; also the three youths,
unharmed, in the furnace at Babylon, from a fragment of
a sarcophagus ; they are represented in the attitude of
prayer, before referred to [97] ; and Elijah's triumphant
entry into heaven in a chariot, his mantle, disproportionate
in size, descending to Elisha, who, to tell the story of his
comparative youth, is represented as a child [95]. This
latter subject exhibits great boldness of treatment as a
work of art. All these subjects are of a cheerful and
encouraging class. " The ancient Church never represented scenes of a painful character : the deliverance of a
Jew from the lions of Babylon was preferred to the destruction of a Christian by those of the Colosseum ; and
the three Hebrews preserved from the rage of Nebuchad-
nezzar was a more consolatory subject than the victims of
Neronian cruelty wrapped in pitchcloth, and used as
torches to illuminate the circus."*

And now to pass from the Old Testament to the *New :*
there is no occasion to reiterate the observations made,
for they are also applicable here. The raising of Lazarus
from the dead is a very frequent subject upon sarcophagi ;
its appropriateness is at once apparent. Here is an instance [95] in which the Roman-shaped tomb and the
mummy of Lazarus after the Egyptian fashion, show the
Pagan artist, or, at all events, Pagan ideas. At the feet
of the Saviour is a figure, either Mary the sister of

* " Church in the Catacombs," p. 311.

Lazarus, or it may possibly be intended to represent the latter, "bound hand and foot with grave-clothes."

A great variety of our Lord's miracles are found represented. Here are two [99], intended for the miracles of the multiplication of the loaves and fishes, and changing of the water into wine at Cana of Galilee.

It was one of the arguments of the infidel school of the last century, that if the early Christians had believed in the miracles of Christ, they would more frequently have appealed to them in their controversies with their Pagan adversaries. Much learning and ingenuity is exercised, upon the reply to this objection, by Dr. Paley, in his "Evidences of the Truth of Christianity."* Had the Doctor been as well acquainted with the Christian Catacombs as some are in the present day, he might have spared himself some labour, and cut very short the argument, by pointing to the *sculptured* "*evidences*" cut in the rock with an iron pen for ever.

Christ in his Scripture character of the "Good Shepherd," is a very favourite decoration of the Catacombs. In three representations which I show you, the subject is slightly varied [96]. He is represented carrying home the lost, the tender, or the weakly sheep. He is habited in the Roman dress. In one case the Pagan "Pan's pipes" are represented to indicate his office; in another you will notice the monogram on the head, to remove all doubt as to the person intended. You will observe, also, the great diversity of age and personal appearance in these representations. It is evident that the Christians of the early Church never attempted any likeness of their Divine Master, of whose appearance, although traditional

* Part III. chap. v.

95

THE RAISING OF LAZARUS, & ELIJAH TRANSLATED.

96

THE GOOD SHEPHERD.

accounts may have been transmitted, no reliable likeness had been preserved.

As with regard to their own sufferings, so the early Christians appear to have been equally indisposed to dwell upon those of their Lord. The best and most plausible reason which can be assigned for this conduct is, that the Christians of that day regarded, more than we have done in after ages, the sufferings of Christ and of his people as matter for glorying. The Apostles counted themselves happy that they were permitted to suffer persecution for the sake of their crucified Saviour; and Paul could exclaim, " God forbid that I should glory, save in the cross of our Lord Jesus Christ!" They looked upon such subjects in a cheerful light, as matters for rejoicing; it was a much later and colder age which introduced the painful representations of the sufferings of Christ's human nature, to aid flagging and almost expiring faith.

Amongst the very few allusions to the last hours of our Lord upon earth are two, which I show you [97, 98] : one of them represents Pilate, his wife, and an attendant; the former is washing his hands after the Oriental mode, as related by Matthew (chap. xxvii. 24). The subject would seem, as Dr. Maitland suggests, to have reference to the declaration of our Lord's freedom from guilt, " I am innocent of the blood of this *just* person;" and by inference, the innocence of the Christians, as it concerned the charge of treason brought against them by their Pagan persecutors.

The other sculpture is from a sarcophagus, the subject being Peter denying his Master, and the cock crowing. This work of art is of a date somewhat later than the time of Constantine, as one of the Roman Basilicæ, or courts of Justice—made over to the use of the Christians

in that reign as places of worship,—appears in the background. These buildings serve to point out the origin
of ecclesiastical arrangements which have since then come
very generally into use.*

Although incidentally referred to, as in the two cases
pointed out, it does not appear that the early Christians
ever took pleasure in portraying the *actual* scenes of suffering through which their Lord and Saviour passed. It
is uncertain whether this arose from a repugnance to
represent scenes in which his human form must have
figured prominently, and which, considering also his
divine nature, prompted by reverent feelings, they shrunk
from attempting, or whether, as has been already suggested, they overlooked to a great extent the sufferings
of Christ in their earnest appreciation of the glory that
followed.

The monogram, already explained, or a cross of two
lines scratched on a gravestone, were at first the simple
modes adopted for expressing faith in a crucified Lord.
The transition from the simple to the elaborate, the
peaceful to the horrible, is well traced in the following
extracts :—" The primitive symbols were also as rudi-
mentary as they were cheerful : *two crossed lines* recorded
the whole story of the Passion. In course of time, faith
begins to cool; the sculptor finds it necessary to suggest
rather more strongly the meaning of the symbol. About

---

* The origin of the arrangements of ecclesiastical architecture
will be found fully and satisfactorily examined in Dr. Maitland's
" Church in the Catacombs," 2nd edit., pp. 339—349. The Catacomb chapel and the Roman court of law having each of them
contributed its share towards the development of church architecture, this point was reached in the fourth century; towers and
spires were added at a later date.

99

.MIRACLES OF OUR LORD.

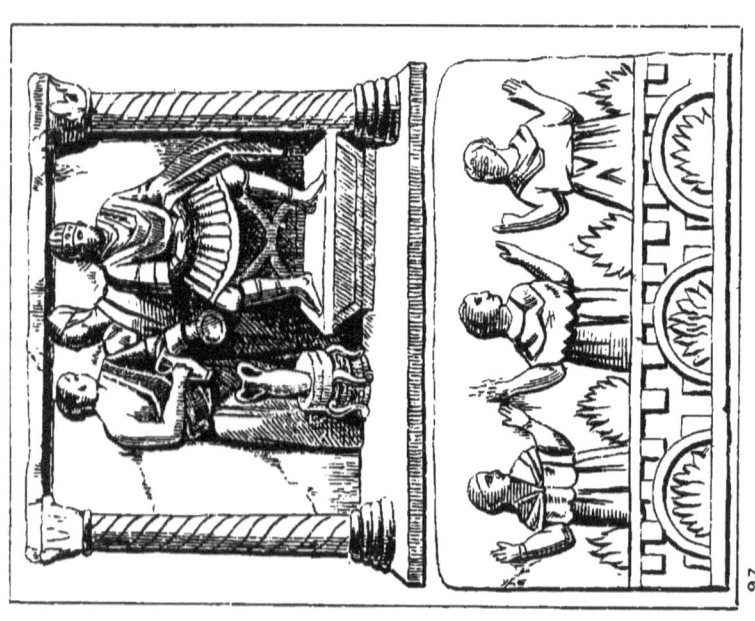

PILATE WASHING HANDS.
THE THREE YOUTHS IN THE FURNACE.

the year 400, there appears at the foot of the cross *a white lamb ;* by the help of this sacrificial emblem, mankind contrives to remember the atonement for three hundred years longer. In the year 706 the Quinisextan Council took away the lamb,* and painted in its place *a living man,* at first seen standing beneath the cross, with arms extended as if in prayer. This affecting representation seems to have lasted out that century. In the ninth the painter raised Christ to the transverse beam ; the darkened sun and moon now appear above the cross ; but He still prays with hands unconfined. In the tenth century Christ is *first represented as dead,* the nails being driven into the hands and feet. About the thirteenth the head drops on one side. * * * The painter having developed the symbol of the Passion from the simple cross to the complete painting, was followed by the sculptor, who beginning in the eleventh century with a mere bas-relief, in the fourteenth arrived at the *portable crucifix. This was material enough : faith had been superseded by sight, and sight by touch.*"† We learn in passing what I have before hinted at, the *danger of employing symbols in relation to Divine things ;* there is a tendency in man, evidenced by his history in all ages, to abuse the use of symbols and incur peril of idolatry.

I close this reference to the fine arts of the Catacombs with a quotation, which well and concisely sums up all that I have stated. "On the whole, it may be safely assumed that the Catacombs, destined to be the sepulchre

---

* 82nd Canon.

† The symbolism was further degraded, and the *living crucifix,* with its "*stigmata,*" or five wounds, was eventually produced by the Church of Rome.—The "Church in the Catacombs," pp. 204 —208.

of the first Christians, for long periods peopled by martyrs, decorated during the persecutions of the Church
and under the immediate dominion of sad thoughts and
agonizing duties, do really offer on all sides nothing but
heroism in the historical pictures, and in the purely orna-
mental part nothing but graceful and cheering subjects ;
as representations of the vintage, of pastoral scenes, of
love-feasts, of fruits, flowers, palm-branches, laurel crowns,
lambs, doves, and does ; in a word, *nothing but what
suggests a feeling of joyous innocence—such as the world
knew when it was young—and charity, such as the Lamb
of God first brought into the world.* Here are no figures
agonizing on the cross, no pictures of the cross and
passion, the agony and bloody sweat, the precious death
and burial. For the crucifixion you must go to other
cemeteries, which were *not* decorated in the first ages of
Christianity. In the midst of their agitated lives, and in
contemplation of a painful death, these first converts of
the faith regarded the grave only as *a sure and short
road to eternal happiness.* Far from associating with it
images of torture and horror, they endeavoured to enliven
the tomb with bright and cheerful colours ; to present
death under the most agreeable symbols, to wreathe it
with foliage and flowers. In these dark crypts, among
all these funereal fragments and remnants of the dead,
you see no sinister symbol, no image of distress and
mourning, no sign of resentment, no expression of hatred
or revenge ; on the contrary, all these objects breathe
sentiments of composure, gentleness, affection, and brotherly love. * * * Also in the first churches, when
pictures were attempted upon the walls or cupolas, the
subjects were all taken from Holy Writ. The painters
who worked above ground had the same source of inspi-

155

ration as the artists who decorated these Catacombs;
and that source was the BIBLE."*

That word reminds me of the point at which we had
arrived in tracing the corruption of Christianity in the
Romish system, when I commenced the digression upon
the *fine arts* in the Catacombs.

I think I may now return to our argument, and ask
you whether, in withholding the Scriptures from the
people, and keeping them in ignorance of that which is
the Christian's charter—the inspired Word of God—the
Church of Rome has not again afforded evidence that she
has substituted a debased for a primitive and pure Christianity; the Scriptures themselves, the early Christian
writers, and the Catacombs of Rome being our witnesses?†

Before leaving the subject of the *fine arts* in the
Catacombs, one more testimony they will afford against a
practice which Rome has introduced to her infinite dishonour, that of representing, like her Pagan predecessors,

* Macfarlane's "Catacombs of Rome," pp. 124—26.

† Further evidence of the possession of the Scriptures by the
early Christians is to be found in the fact that there were, in times
of persecution, persons who gave them up, who were termed *traditors* accordingly, *i.e.*, traitors to God, who had committed to
their custody a sacred gift. *Traditors* were, by their act, considered as lapsed persons, that is, apostates from Christianity. At
a synod held at Cirta, in Numidia, for instance, one Paul was
deposed from his office as a *traditor*, and upon proceeding to con-
secrate a successor, it appeared, unhappily, that others present
had committed the same crime. Optatus de Schismat. Donatist.
lib. i. p. 39; Augustine Cont. Cresc., lib. iii. cap. 26—28. Many
other references to the offence of giving up the Scriptures are
contained in the writings concerning the early Church. See also
the testimony of Fenelon (a Roman Catholic), *Œuvres Spirituels*,
tom. iv., p. 241.

the *great God* — the eternal, immortal, and invisible
Jehovah — *under the form of " corruptible man."* The
early Christians, although with all reverence and delicacy
of feeling they portrayed their Lord in human form,
never ventured to design God the Father in the likeness
of flesh. In cases in which the subject required allusion
to the interference of God, they hinted at it by intro-
ducing a symbolical hand. Here are two instances
[100] : in one of which Moses is represented taking the
tables of the Law from a hand veiled in " clouds and
darkness ;" in the other, the outstretched hand of God is
represented as interposing to stay the sacrifice of Isaac
by the patriarch Abraham. This symbolic hand became
the germ from which sprang the disregard of the Second
Commandment, which grew with the growth of Romish
corruption, until it became so flagrant and apparent, that
it became necessary for that Church to drop, as she did,
the command from the Decalogue. There is found in a
French MS. of the ninth century, a representation of
God the Father as an *aged man*—precisely the Jupiter of
the Pagans revived. In two MSS. of the Apocalypse, of
the fourteenth century, one of which is in the British
Museum, there appear representations of Christ, as a
lamb standing on its hind legs, and taking the book with
the seven seals from " Him that sat upon the throne,"
represented in each case as a *man*. These subjects would
be ridiculous if they were not painfully blasphemous ; it
is quite out of the question affording illustrations of
them.* In later times this offence became more frequent;
and in Roman Catholic churches both pictures and carvings
to this hour afford evidence that God's laws are dis-

* See Twining's " Symbols and Emblems," Plate xi., figs.
3 and 5.

98

PETER DENIES HIS LORD.

100

ABRAHAM & ISAAC.   MOSES & THE LAW.

regarded and set at nought in this, as in other respects. If any of you were to cross the Channel to Calais, and visit there the chief church, you would see a representation of the Virgin Mary as a young woman, Christ as a young man, and the Eternal Father as an old man, and the Holy Spirit as a dove. You will picture to yourselves that the Virgin would be represented as offering adoration to the representations of the persons in the Trinity—no such thing ; *the Divine persons are crowning the head of the Virgin.* And so at Paris, in the church called " The Madeleine," God the Father is represented as *a man* reclining on a couch. The Eternal JEHOVAH, who " fainteth not, neither is weary,"* is actually represented *taking rest after the fatigues of creation ! !* Wherein is such a system better than that of the Pagans of old? Is not that a deeply-debased Christianity, if Christianity it can be called, which substitutes such religion for the spiritual worship of a Spirit God. In this respect also I would have you notice that the Catacombs witness clearly against Romanism that it is neither primitive nor pure.

One more illustration of my argument, and I conclude. In nothing was the religion of Jesus Christ more distinguished from all that the world had then known of religion, than in its *loving* and *blessing* spirit. Its existence was based upon an act of love unparalleled. In love to God and to human nature all its laws are included and summed up. Those laws, as expounded by their Great Author, forbade cursing, and enjoined blessing ; " BLESS, and CURSE NOT." With severity of reproof unusual with the meek and gentle Saviour, He condemned the *spirit of persecution* when it appeared in the behaviour of his dis-

* Isaiah xl. 28.

ciples. " Ye know not what manner of spirit ye are of;
for the Son of Man is not come to destroy men's lives, but to
save them,"* was his reply, when they suggested the propagation of his Gospel by other means than by kindly
persuasion and the force of Christian example.
This is not the spirit in which his religion has been
set before the world by the recent Church of Rome. Alas !
in this respect especially, she has shown herself the parent
of unfaithful daughters,† who have often followed her
pernicious example, and persecuted those who differed
from themselves. But Rome stands pre-eminently con-
spicuous as a *cursing* and a *persecuting* Church; she
curses systematically, awfully, in terms which I dare not
repeat to you. And with respect to persecution and
blood-shedding, she has emulated her Pagan predecessors,
and earned for herself the character accorded to her in
Inspired Writ, " *drunken with the blood of the saints.*"
It would weary you were I to attempt even to enumerate
the slaughter she has committed in the name of the religion of the loving Jesus. In the valleys of Piedmont,
Switzerland, the Tyrol, and Bohemia, the blood of Albi-
genses, Vaudois, Waldenses, and others who protested
against Rome's corruptions, was poured out like water.
In the sixteenth century, France affords an illustration of
the fiendish spirit of persecution; men, women, and
children were indiscriminately slaughtered by the sword,
by hanging, roasting over slow fires, cast from high rocks,
or upon pikes. Sucking infants, who could not know
their right hand from their left, were not spared, but
killed with bludgeons before the eyes of their mothers;

* Luke ix. 55, 56.
† " The Mother of Harlots," or unfaithfulness, she is called in
Holy Writ.

nor did the sex of woman shield her. On one occasion five hundred women were forced into a barn, which was set on fire, and all were destroyed. This was but desultory and ineffectual persecution; a design was formed, deliberately, for the utter extinction of pure religion in France, and carried out on the 24th August, 1572, and lasted seven days. It is known by the name of the Massacre of St. Bartholomew; more than 5000 persons were slaughtered in Paris, and at least 20,000 more in other parts of France. The Pope rejoiced in this bloody deed, publicly returned thanks to God for its success, and congratulated the French king on the accomplishment of a purpose *" so long meditated and so happily executed."* He even struck a medal, on which he represented himself, Gregory XIII., on the obverse, and on the reverse the Massacre, with the inscription, " THE SLAUGHTER OF THE HUGONOTS, 1572."* Our own country has not escaped, although it has been, by God's mercy, visited more leniently than others. The Netherlands were literally drenched in blood. The Duke of Alva boasted of having put to death 18,000 Protestants in six weeks, and the whole number massacred in that country, solely on account of their religion, fell little short, if at all, of 100,000. In Italy, Spain, Portugal, Mexico, turn where you will, you will read the history of Rome's authority in letters of blood.

The Inquisition—an institution established to put a stop to the Reformation—has, since its establishment, sacrificed its hundreds of thousands, or, as some writers assert, its millions of victims; the total will never be

* This medal is described in the "Numismata Pontificum Romanorum," tom. i. p. 336.

known until "the earth shall disclose her blood, and no
more cover her slain." Carrying on its proceedings in
darkness and secresy—violating the sanctity of domestic
life, and even of connubial attachment, in obtaining its
victims—condemning without a charge, and often without
a hearing—by fearful tortures, extorting evidence to incul-
pate and bring into the same condemnation those who are
nearest in relationship or dearest in affection—it appears,
in my humble judgment, the masterpiece of Satan's
cruelty; permitted to exist only to warn us to "come
out of" and keep clear of Rome and her system. And
think not, my friends, to deceive yourselves by saying,
" This is an old story, and a state of things long past and
gone." Tell me *which of the persecuting and cursing
canons of Rome has been repealed,* and my charity will be
prepared to admit that she has changed her character;
let me see that, although unrepealed, she has ceased to·
use them, and I will, even then, admit it. But her bloody
statutes are on her books; her persecuting pictures adorn
the walls of the Pope's palace; her sanguinary medals are
in the Pope's collection; and blood is even now on her
hands in the middle of the nineteenth century. England
was once a persecutor for conscience sake. On her statute
books were laws enjoining the burning of heretics; the
imprisonment, multilation, and execution of non-con-
formists; she sanctioned the use of the torture to extort
evidence. Had these laws remained unrepealed, how
could she have replied to the charge of persecution and
cruelty? But Rome, in this respect, since she fell, is
unchanged and unchanging. Even while I address you,
her recognized organs are justifying persecution, and in-
timating that she still thirsts for blood. I will not read to
you what Protestants say of Rome, but I will read what

Rome, speaking in the "Univers," her recognized organ on the Continent, says about us.*

"A heretic, examined and convicted by the Church, used to be delivered over to the secular power and punished with *death*. Nothing has ever appeared to us more natural or more necessary. More than 100,000 perished in consequence of the heresy of Wicliffe; a still greater number by that of John Huss; *it would not be possible to calculate the bloodshed caused by the heresy of Luther, and it is not yet over. After three centuries, we are at the* EVE OF A RECOMMENCEMENT."

And now, what say the Catacombs to the spirit of their Christian occupants? Surely, if ever there were men entitled to curse, to retaliate, and to revenge, it was these poor outcasts; proscribed for no crime, persecuted and put to death, without law, without trial, and without mercy. But mark the fact, not one word of hatred, revenge, dislike, is ever expressed against their persecutors and enemies; not even a stray scrawl is to be found on the walls of their prison, implying a desire to retaliate, to curse, or to avenge. Such inscriptions as the following have been found, but they breathe a different spirit :—

MAXIMINUS, WHO LIVED XXIII YEARS; FRIEND OF ALL MEN.

IN CHRIST. ON THE FIFTH BEFORE THE KALENDS OF NOVEMBER SLEPT GORGONIUS, FRIEND OF ALL, AND ENEMY OF NONE.

The history of their triumph under Constantine tells the same tale. When released from the persecutions of

* Vide "L'Univers," August, 1851. Also articles written in August, 1872, the tercentenary of the massacre of St. Bartholomew, justifying that act.

the Pagans, and armed with the powers of the State, they turned not those powers against their enemies and persecutors; they were more busied in the manumission of slaves, and in putting down the bloody games of the circus, than in recording or revenging the injuries they had received. Would that it were in the power of the historian to trace the same line of conduct in after times !

Again, I ask, am I not justified in asserting that Christianity has been corrupted; that the Romish system has largely borrowed the cursing, persecuting, and blood-thirsty spirit of Paganism? that for the Christian religion of the Catacombs and the Bible, there has been sub-tituted a false, a spurious imitation, which does not bear the impress of the Divine original?

To the objection, " *If Christianity is a Divine institu-tion and remedy, why has it not effected more completely its mission by removing evils which still afflict our world?* " I have replied, " BECAUSE CHRISTIANITY WAS CORRUPTED, AND IS, TO A GREAT EXTENT, CORRUPTED STILL." Had time permitted, the proof could have been much extended, but I have preferred confining myself to the fundamental errors of the system; all others matters are mere accessories and sequences. I have made plain, I trust, that these fundamental corruptions consist in a derogation from the honour, a usurpation of the rights of the Lord Jesus Christ, by setting aside his teaching and infringing upon his various offices : of Priest, by sub-stituting an unauthorized priesthood; of Saviour, by supplying a supplementary sacrifice; of Mediator, by adding a host of unnecessary intercessors; of Prophet, by withholding the inspired Word of God. And, as a consequence, Rome having reverted to the Pagan system in all these respects, she has naturally come to display the worst features of Pagan spirit.

WHY this corruption of truth, and consequent suspension of the hopes of the world, has been permitted, I again repeat it is not for *us* to determine. Suffice it to reply, that it was *foreknown* and clearly *predicted*, and that the true Church of Christ, from the days of the Apostles to this hour, has known the fact, and been consoled also by the knowledge that the destruction of the system is also determined upon, and that it will be sudden, fearful, and complete.*

In this view of the subject, how important is it for us to understand clearly the principles of the system, so as to keep clear of its corruptions; for the Word of inspiration, in telling of its coming judgment, informs us also of a " voice" which is loudly to sound, and which even my feeble and unworthy utterance may be permitted even now to swell : " *Come out of her, my people, that ye be not partakers of her sins, and that ye receive not of her plagues.*" †

The number of those who still submit themselves to the teachings of Rome is very great, and she has many admirers who in secret bow the knee to her without openly professing it. This being so, it may be asked by some of you, "How comes it that so many are deceived, and

---

* See "Apostolic School of Prophetic Interpretation," by Dr. Maitland, in which the belief that Rome is the predicted Babylon of the Apocalypse is shown to have been the faith of the Christian Church *in every age.*

† Rev. xviii. 4.

claim for Romanism that it is *primitive, holy, universal, and apostolic?*"

I must first remind you that a numerical majority (even if Rome possessed it) could not determine a question of truth or error. When Christianity arrived in the world, Paganism was all but universal: that fact did not, however, prove Paganism true and Christianity false. At the present moment it is believed that the worshippers of Buddha in India and China outnumber the professors of any other religious sect, but you will perceive that that fact cannot determine the truth of Buddhism. Thus the number of those who are deceived by error cannot convert error into truth. And so with regard to pertinacious reiteration of a statement: a falsehood, however often repeated, is a falsehood still. The Ephesians of old continued by the space of two hours to reiterate "Great is Diana of the Ephesians," without establishing the dignity of their imaginary divinity. The progress of truth is ever slow, while error moves with rapid steps: the reason is obvious; error is seized upon by those who ask no evidence, while the searchers after truth, hitherto a small minority of mankind, adopt it only after deliberate examination.

I will tell you, however, another secret of the power of Romanism. I have said that a falsehood, however often reiterated, can never become truth; but it is also a lamentable fact, that by the *constant reiteration of a falsehood, it acquires in our unthinking world the force of truth.* This is the reason why the system I speak of has so many adherents, notwithstanding its flagrant departures from primitive and pure Christianity. It is unhappily the case in this world of ours, both in commerce and in religion, that the corrupted, debased, adulterated article passes too frequently for the genuine and the pure, upon the word of the loudest and boldest asseverator.

This tendency in falsehood to pass unchallenged and the true reason of its success are so well stated by a living poet, that I cannot forbear quoting him :—

> "Build a lie—yes, build a lie,
>   A large one—be not over tender;
> Give it a form, and raise it high,
>   That all the world may see its splendour;
> Then launch it like a mighty ship
>   On the restless sea of men's opinion,
> And the ship shall sail before the gale
>   Endued with motion and dominion.
>
> Though storms may batter it evermore,
>   Though angry lightnings flash around it,
> Though whirlwinds rave, and whirlpools roar,
>   To overwhelm and to confound it,
> The ship shall ride, all wrath of time
>   And hostile elements defying :
> The winds of Truth are doubtless strong,
>   But great 's the buoyancy of lying.
>
> And though the ship grow old at last,
>   Leaky, and water-logged, and crazy,
> Yet still the hulk endures the blast,
>   And fears no weather, rough or hazy ;
> For should she sink, she'll rise again,
>   No strength her rotten planks shall sever ;
> *Give her but size and the worst of lies*
>   *May float about the world for ever."* *

I must, however, conclude with a remark or two

* Dr. Mackay.

by way of lessons which we may derive from the subject
we have been considering.

First. I will suggest another answer with which, from
to-night, you may be furnished, when Romanists ask you,
as they are very fond of doing in their ignorance, "Where
was your religion before the Reformation?" There have
been two answers usually given to this question; one of
them distinguished by its wit, and the other by its sound-
ness. The first reply is, in fact, a counter-question—
"Where was your face this morning, before you washed
it?" Now, this reply I do *not* recommend you to use. I
would rather advise you to reply, "It was in the New
Testament;" where, if your faith be sound, it will
assuredly be found. But from to-night you can reply
also, "*It was in the Catacombs of Rome.*" There was
primitive and pure Christianity, and that will be *primitive,
holy, universal,* and *apostolic* religion which resembles it.

Then, secondly, notice the wise providence of God
with regard to the preservation of the antiquities of the
Catacombs. Hidden from the world during a thousand
years, they came forth just as the corruption of Rome was
complete and the reformation from error commenced, as
important witnesses in the controversy which was henceforth to be maintained; but the state of learning was not
then favourable for the full development of their testimony. The Popes, however, preserved the stones in
their museum; eminent antiquarians (Roman Catholics)
copied and published the inscriptions, and thus preserved
them from being lost, until this day, when the enemy
"coming in like a flood," Christians are permitted to lift

them up as a standard against error and false religion.
This is not the first time in the world's history that a
culprit has treasured up the evidence which has ultimately
proved the means of his conviction.

Lastly. *If you would know Christianity, learn it from
the Bible.* Which of you, having the option of drinking
at the fountain-head of the river, or of slaking your
thirst from its turbid and polluted waves after it has
scoured some mighty city, would not rather prefer the
pure crystal draught from the unpolluted source ? Study,
then, this Divine institution, where its features are truth-
fully delineated in the pages which record the words and
actions of its Divine Founder, and attend the teaching of
those who draw water the purest from these " wells of
salvation." Do not be so unwise or so unjust as to condemn that which is in itself pure and holy, and calculated
to make you unspeakably happy, because some have forged
counterfeits, and passed them for the true. You act not
so with respect to the secular affairs of life. Money still
possesses its value, and fine gold is still esteemed by you,
notwithstanding it is sometimes counterfeited by baser
metal. Pictures by eminent artists command and maintain their price, even though copies, unworthy of the
original, are abroad. Oh! that it were thus with regard
to the more important concerns of our souls. We take
up, unthinkingly and without examination, anything pre-
sented to us as the religion of Christ, and either reject it
altogether, because of some unattractive and repulsive
feature which belongs not to it, or, if receiving it, we
render homage to some distorted representation, to the
dishonour of the Divine Originator.

May it be your lot and mine, so to learn Christ from the inspired reflection He has left behind Him, that " we all, with open face beholding as in a glass the glory of the Lord, may be changed into the same likeness from glory to glory, even as by the Spirit of the Lord."*

* 2 Cor. iii. 18.

Simmons & Botten, Printers, Shoe Lane, E.C.

LIST OF DIAGRAMS

FOR THE

ILLUSTRATION OF LECTURES,

PUBLISHED BY THE WORKING MEN'S EDUCATIONAL UNION,

28, PATERNOSTER ROW, E.C. W. THORN, DEPOSITARY.

₊ These Diagrams are 3 feet by 4 feet in area; printed on cloth; adapted for distant inspection; coloured for gas or candle-light; and are both durable and portable. They may be had singly or in sets.

Price 3s. each Diagram; double, treble, and quadruple sizes in proportion.

THE USUAL ALLOWANCES TO SUBSCRIBERS AND THE TRADE.

DIAGRAM   **(Physiology.)**

No. 54 and 55   Human Skeleton (*double size*, 6 feet by 4 feet).
   56   Organs of Mastication, Deglutition, &c.
   57   Organs of Digestion,—gullet, stomach, &c.
   58   Organs of Circulation,—heart, showing valves, &c.
   59   Organs of Circulation and Respiration.
   60   Organs of Sensation,—brain, nerves, &c.
   61   The Skin, its Structure and Appendages.
   62   Effects of Tight Lacing.
   63   Effects of Intemperate Use of Alcoholic Liquors.
      See also Nos. 487 to 491.

(Houses in the East.)
   64   Booths made of Branches—Feast of Tabernacles.
   65   Progress of Architecture—Huts, Capitals, &c.
   66   Windows—Balconies, Kiosks, &c , of Eastern Houses.
   67   Oriental Doors (Arabic) with writing thereon.
   68   Ground Plan and Section of Oriental House.
   69   Court of Oriental House,—interior view.
   70   Roofs of ditto—House-tops, Dome, and Minaret.
   71   Tents, various; and Booth of Hurdle-work.
   72   Cave-dwelling—interior.
   73   Rock-dwellings in Edom or Petra—exterior.

(Cruelties of Idolatry, Pagan Practices.)
   74   Offering Children to Moloch.
   75   Druid Sacrifice as described by Cæsar.
   76   Child Murder in Indian Temple.
   77   Hindoo Suttee, or Widow-burning.
   78   Dying Gladiator in the Colosseum.
   79   Gladiatorial Combat—Bas-reliefs from Pompeii.
      See also Nos. 272 and 275.

DIAGRAM (**The Catacombs at Rome, and Early Christianity.**)
No. 80 Gallery, with Tombs, in the Catacombs at Rome.
81 Tombs and Slabs in ditto.
82 Fossors—Inscriptions relating to, in ditto.
83 Phonetic Symbols, referring to names in ditto.
84 Ditto—referring to Trades and Occupations.
85 Ditto   ditto
86 Religious Symbols—Monogram of Christ.
87 Sundries—Fish Symbol—Crown and Palms, &c.
88 Religious Symbols—Doves, Ship, Anchor.
89 Inscriptions—Christian and Pagan contrasted.
90 Epitaphs of Four Martyrs.
91 Praying Figures—Bellicia and the Apostle Paul.
92 Painting of Love Feast, and Cups
93 Bas-reliefs—1, Noah and Jonah ; 2, Jonah.
94 Fresco Painting—Daniel and the Lions.
95 Bas-reliefs—1, Raising of Lazarus ; 2, Elijah's Translation.
96 Representations of "the Good Shepherd."
97 Bas-reliefs—Pilate Washing his Hands ; Shadrach, Meshach, and
      Abednego, in the " Fiery Furnace."
98 Bas-relief—Peter Denying his Lord.
99 Paintings—Miracle of Loaves and Fishes, ditto of Water changed
      into Wine.
100 Bas-reliefs—Abraham and Isaac ; Moses receiving the Tables of
      the Law.

(Mechanics.)
101 The Lever and its Applications.
102 The Pulley, the Wheel and Axle
103 The Inclined Plane, Wedge, and Screw.

(Optics—The Telescope.)
104 The Human Eye.
105 Refraction of Light, with Section of Lenses.
106 Refracting Telescopes—The Galilean and the Terrestrial.
107 Great Refracting Telescope at Cambridge
108 Reflecting Telescopes—The Newtonian and the Cassegrainian.
109 Lord Rosse's Great Reflecting Telescope.

(Astronomy—The Nebulæ.)
110 Various forms of Nebulæ.
111 The Nebula in Hercules.
112 The Dumb Bell Nebula.
113 The Crab Nebula
114 and 115 The Whirlpool, or Spiral Nebula, *double size*.

(Optics—The Microscope.)
116 External View of a Compound Microscope.
117 Internal Arrangement of its Lenses
118 Works of Nature and of Art, contrasted.
119 Various Objects Magnified.
120 Cheese Mite, Crustaceous Animalcules, &c.
121 Various Animalcules.

DIAGRAM   **(Life in Australia.)**

No. 121 · The Voyage—Table Mountain, Cape of Good Hope.
   122   Emigrant Ship arriving at Sydney.
   123   Australian Farm, Sheep Washing.
   124   Going to the Diggings.
   125   Gold Washing at ditto.
   126   Escort of Gold; Native Police.
   128   Natives and Native Hut.
   129   Corrobory, or Dance of Natives.
   130   ‾Animals and Birds of Australia.
   131   Trees and Plants of Australia.

(Homes in the East and Domestic Arrangements.
   132   Sitting Postures amongst Orientals.
   133   Throne and Chairs—Assyria.
   134   Throne and Chairs—Egypt.
   135   Tables from Egypt and Assyria.
   136   Washing Hands—Oriental Method.
   137   Modes of Eating in the East.
   138   Sleeping Accommodations—Oriental.
   139   Mode of Grinding Corn in the East.
   140   Oriental Lamps and Oven.
   141   Water and Wine Skins in the East.

(Astronomy—Comet.)
   142   Two Views of the Comet of 1853.
         See also No. 251.

(Locomotion—Travelling in the Old Times.)
   143   Saxon Chariots or Wheel Beds.
   144   Saxon Waggon, and Lady on Horseback.
   145   Female Horsemanship in the 15th Century.
   146   Horse Litter of 14th Century.
   147   Queen Isabella of France in her State Litter.
   148   Travelling Waggon of 14th Century.
   149   Pack Horses and Drivers.
   150   State Coaches of Queen Elizabeth and her Attendant
   151   Coaches of 1616 and 1696.
   152   Carriages of the Reign of Queen Anne.
   153   Modern Stage Coach.
   154   Railway Train—Night.

(For Illustration of High Numbers in Astronomy
   155   One Million Points, 10 ft. by 10 ft.

(Ruins of Nineveh.)
   156   Human-headed Winged Lion, from Nineveh.
   157   Slab from Nineveh, Sennacherib before Lachish.
   158   Architectural Ornaments, &c.
   159   Assyrian Temple, Nimroud.
   160   Pottery, Helmets, &c.
   161   Jewish Captives, imploring mercy of Sennacherib.
   162   Eagle-headed Human Figure, Nisroch.
   163   Nimrod, the "Mighty Hunter."
   164   King in War Chariot, fording a River.
   165   Transport of Winged Bull by Assyrians.
   166   King Hunting Lions, Religious Symbols.
   167   Sieges, with Mounds, Battering Ram, &c.

DIAGRAM **(Ruins of Nineveh** --*continued.*)

No. 168 Transport of Winged Bull, by Mr. Layard ; Mound of Nimroud.
169 Banquet of Wine.
170 Heads of Slain counted.
171 Map of the Tigris, with Site of Nineveh.
172 Cruelty to Captives, Tongues torn out, &c.
173 Restored Exterior of Assyrian Palace.
174 Archive or Record Chamber at Kouyunjik.
175 Eyes of Captive put out by King of Assyria.

(The Literary History of the Bible.)

176 Writing on Stone—The Rosetta Stone.
177 Picture Writing from Karnak, Thebes.
178 Ancient MSS. and Writing Materials.
179 Multiplication of Copies—Scriptorium and Scribe.
180 Multiplication of Copies—Printing Press.
181 The Burnt Roll, or the Scriptures destroyed.
182 Bible Burning at Paul's Cross.
183 Wycliff before Archbishop Courtenay.
184 The Bible Chained, as read in the Crypt of St. Paul's.
185 The Death of the Venerable Bede.
186 Luther finding the Bible in the Library at Erfurt.
187 Luther Translating the Bible into German.
188 Search for New Testaments at Oxford.
189 Bible Society's House and Warehouse.
190 Interior View of St. Paul's, Jubilee of Bible Society.
See also No. 199, and Nos. 492 to 498.

(The Reformation in England.)

191 Cardinal Wolsey going in Procession to the King's Chapel.
192 Burning of John Brown the Martyr's Feet.
193 Worshippers at the Altars of St. Thomas and the Virgin.
194 Exposure of the Inner Machinery of the Rood of Kent.
195 Legates Presiding at the Court for Divorce of Queen Catherine.
196 Monks Carousing at Newstead Abbey.
197 Parliament submitting to Cardinal Pole.
198 Burning of Ridley and Latimer at Oxford.
199 The Bible and the Printing Press.

(Geology.)

200, 201, 202 *Triple size.* Section of the Earth's Crust.
203 Order of the Various Geological Systems and Strata.
204 Fossils of the Clay-slate, Grauwacke, and Silurian Systems.
205 Section of the London Basin, with Artesian Well.
206 Fossils of the Devonian, or old Red Sandstone.
207 Fossils of the Carboniferous System.
208 Fossils of the New Red (Triassic) System.
209 Fossil Flora of the Oolite and immediately Antecedent Systems.
210 Fossil Shells and Fruit from the Lias, Oolite, and Wealden.
211 Fossil Saurians from the Oolite.
212 Fossils of the Chalk Formation.
213 Fossils of the Tertiary Series.
214 Fossils of the Superficial Strata.
See also No. 448 ; also Nos. 234 to 239.

6

DIAGRAM   **(The Fulfilled Prophecies.)**

No. 215   The Arabs ; their wild independence.
216   The Arabs ; Dwellings in Tents.
217   View of the Ruins of Petra (Edom).
218   Babylon—the Birs Nimroud.
219   Babylon—the Mujelibe, &c.
220   Tyre, Ruins of, from a Photograph.
221   Tyre, View of the Port.
222   Egypt, her desolation—Thebes or No.
223   Egypt, Sole Remains of On, or Heliopolis.
224   Jews and Jerusalem—Place of Wailing.
225   Bas-relief from the Arch of Titus at Rome.

(The Seven Churches in Asia.)
226   The Isle of Patmos.
227   Ephesus, Ruins of.
228   Smyrna.
229   Pergamos, Ruins of.
230   Thyatira, Site of.
231   Sardis, Remains of.
232   Philadelphia, Site of.
233   Laodicea, Ruins of.

(Volcanoes and Volcanic Action.)
234   Vesuvius from the Bay of Naples.
235   Stromboli, Night View of, during Eruption.
236   Jorullo, a Crater near Mexico, thrown up September 29, 1759.
237   Crater of Kirauea, Owhyhee.
238   Air Volcanoes, near Carthagena, South America.
239   Geysers, or Boiling Fountains of Iceland.

(Astronomy—The Solar System.)
240, 241   Solar System, Section of, *double size.*
242   The Sun, with comparative sizes of the Planets.
243   Comparative Sizes of the Sun, as seen from various Planets.
244   The Moon, its Telescopic Appearance.
245   Venus, Mercury, Mars.
246   Jupiter and Moons.
247   Saturn, with the other Planets (showing relative sizes).
248   The Tides.
249   The Seasons.
250   Eclipses of Sun and Moon—Law of Shadows.
251   Comets, Various.
     See also Nos. 142, 375, 376, 385, 386, and 402.

(Egypt and its Monuments.)
252   Map of Ancient Egypt, Nubia, &c.
253   Hall of Columns, Karnak, Thebes.
254   Pyramids and Sphinx.
255   Temple of Abou Simbel (Exterior).
256   Temple of Abou Simbel (Interior).
257   The Sitting Statues of Amunoph III.
258   Temple of Edfou (Interior).
259   Tomb at Beni Hassan (Exterior).
260   Tomb of Psammeticus, discovered by Belzoni.
261   Section showing Construction of a Pyramid.

DIAGRAM   **(Natural History—Mammalia.)**

No. 262 Order Bimana—Man.
263 Skeletons of Bimana and Quadrumana.
264 Order Quadrumana—Monkeys.
265 Order Carnaria—Bats.
266 Order Carnaria—Shrew, Mole, &c.
267 Order Carnaria—Lion, Tiger, &c.
268 Order Carnaria—Bear, Wolf, Fox, &c.
269 Order Marsupialia—Kangaroo, &c.
270 Order Rodentia—Squirrel, Hare, Porcupine, &c.
271 Order Edentata—Sloth, Ant-eater, &c.
272 Order Pachydermata—Elephant, Rhinoceros, &c.
273 Order Pachydermata—Horse, Zebra, &c.
274 Order Ruminantia—Deer, Buffalo, &c.
275 Order Ruminantia—Giraffe.
276 Order Cetacea—Whale, Dolphin, &c.
See also Nos. 130, 440, 485, and 486.

(Remains of Pompeii.)
277 Restoration of the City of Pompeii.
278 Remains of the Forum at Pompeii.
279 Circus or Amphitheatre at Pompeii.
280 The Large Theatre at Pompeii.
281 Remains of the Public Baths.
282 Suburban Villa.
283 Restored Interior.
284 Street of Tombs.
285 Baker's Shop, &c.
286 Vessels and Implements.

(Druidism.)
287 Druid Cromlech.
See also Nos. E. H. 3, E. H. 4, and E. H. 8.

(Jewish Tabernacle.
288 Camp of the Israelites (at rest) with the Tabernacle.
288A Ground Plan of the Camp of the Israelites.
289 Interior of the Tabernacle.
290 Brazen (Copper) Altar of Burnt-Offering, &c.
291 Brazen Laver, with Priests Washing.
292 Table of Shewbread, &c.
293 Golden Candlestick, with Ministering Priest, &c.
294 Ark, Mercy-seat, and Cherubim, &c.
295 Order of March of the Israelites.
See also Nos. 321, 478, 480, and 481.

(Cities of Palestine.)
296 Modern Jerusalem, from the Mount of Olives.
297 Bethlehem—Hills of Moab in Background.
298 Nazareth.
299 Tiberias, with the Lake of Galilee.
300 Samaria, Ruins of.
301 Hebron (Mamre, Kirjath-Arba).
302 Bethany.
303 Nablous (Neapolis), anciently Shechem and Sychar.
304 The River Jordan.
See also 344, 480, 481; also large View of Jerusalem, Nos. 325—328.

8

DIAGRAM **(Mountains of the Bible.)** ᛝ
No. 308   Mount Ararat.
309   Mount Lebanon.
310   Mount Sinai, with view of the Convent.
311   Mount Hor, with Tomb of Aaron.
312   Mount Carmel.
313   Mount Tabor.
314   Mount of Olives.
          See also Nos. 368 and 481.

(Types of Scripture.)
315   A Lamb Sacrificed.
316   Noah's Ark.
317   The Priest Melchisedec.
318   The Passover.
319   The Manna.
320   The Rock in Horeb.
321   Aaron, the High Priest.
322   The Brazen Serpent.

(Palestine.)
323, 324   Map of Palestine, *double size.*

(Jerusalem.)
325, 326, 327, 328   View of Modern Jerusalem, from Photograph,
          12 feet by 4 feet.

(Travels of the Apostle Paul.)
329, 330   *Double size* Map of the 1st and 3rd Journeys of the Apostle.
329A, 330A   Map of the 2nd, and of the last Voyage of the Apostle
          Paul, *double size.*
331   Tarsus.
332   Damascus.
333   Antioch, Syria.
334   Antioch, Pisidia.
335   Thessalonica.
336   Athens.
337   Corinth.
338   Miletus.
339   Chart of South Coast, Crete, and View of Fair Havens.
340   Chart and View of St. Paul's Bay, Malta.
341   Puteoli.
342   Rome.
343   Coins, Illustrative of Paul's Travels.
344   Cæsarea Palestina.

(Dr. Livingstone's Researches and Discoveries in Africa.)
345, 346   Map of Dr. Livingstone's Journeys, *double size.*
347   The Victoria Falls.
348   Adventure with a Lion.
349   Trap and Pit for Game.
350   Women with Egg-shells.
351   A Court Presentation.
352   Reception of Missionaries.
353   River Scenery.

(Dr. Livingstone's Researches and Discoveries in Africa—
DIAGRAM   *continued.)*
No. 354   Scenery, with Euphorbias.
    355   Loanda.
    356   Rock Scene.
    357   Adventure with Buffaloes.
    358   Heads of Natives, &c.

(Ancient British History.)
E H 1   Costume of Ancient Britons before Roman Invasion.
E H 2   British War Chariot and Weapons.
B H 3   Arch Druid and Group of Druids.
E H 4   Stonehenge.
B H 5   Landing of Julius Cæsar.
B H 6   Caractacus before Claudius.
E H 7 . Boadicea haranguing the Confederated Britons.
E H 8   Massacre of the Druids.
E H 9   Heads of Roman Emperors.
E H 10   Britons Lamenting the Departure of the Romans.
         See also No. 287.

(The Steam Engine.)
359   Early forms of the Steam Engine.
360   Savery's Engine.
361   Atmospheric Engine.
362   The Boiler.
363   The Cylinder, Piston, Condenser and Parallel Motion.
364   The Governor Crank and Eccentric.
365   Action of ordinary Condensing Engine.
366   Marine (oscillating) Engine.
367   Locomotive Engine.
      See also No. 154.

368   THE MOUNT OF OLIVES *(from a Photograph.)*

(Astronomy—Remarkable Constellations.)
370   Beta Persei.
371   Omicron Ceti.
372   The "Coal Sack" and "Southern Cross."
373   "Hercules."
374   "The Pleides."

(Astronomy—Eclipses.)
375   Total Solar Eclipse.
376   Phases of Solar Eclipse.
      See also No. 250.

382   THE ENGLISH CHURCH AT JERUSALEM *(from a Photograph).*

(Astronomy—Comets.)
385   Comet of 1858.   .
386   Telescopic Appearances of ditto.
      See also Nos. 142, 251, 402.

(The Book [Bible] and its Missions.)
387   Thibet.
388   Burmah and the Missionary Judson.
389   Inscribed Rock of Behistun.

DIAGRAM (**The Book [Bible] and its Missions**—*continued.*)
No. 390 Dagon and Nebo.
391 Constantinople.
392 Colporteur at Daghetejuk.
393 Burning of Hebrew MSS. in Spain.
394 Swiss Colporteur in the Alps.
395 Sketch of Mount Castellazzo and Street of Latour.
396 Night Class for Scripture reading in Poitou.
397 The Nestorian Christians.
398 Sales to Sunday Scholars of Manchester.
399 Swiss Peasants purchasing Bibles.
400 Bible-readers in old St. Giles's.
401 Modern Bible-readers in St. Giles's.

(Astronomy—Comets.)
402 Orbits of Comets and Conic Sections.
     See also 142, 251, 385, 386 and 402.

(The Pilgrim Fathers of New England.)
403 Barrow and Greenwood in the Clink Prison.
404 Martyrdom of John Peury.
405 Map—North East part of England.
406 Site of Manor house at Scrooby.
407 Austerfield Church, Standish Chapel, &c.
408 Delfthaven—Scene on the Maese.
409 The " May-flower " and " Speedwell " in Dartmouth Harbour.
410 Cape Cod Harbour and the " May-flower."
411 Plan of New Plymouth Bay, New England.
412 Relics of the Pilgrim Fathers.

(Ethnology—the Unity of the Human Species.)
413 Skulls of Bimana and Quadrumara.
414 Bases of Skulls—Man and Ourang-Outang.
415 Types of races—Caucasican, Arab, Moor, Mongolian.
416 Types of races—N. American, Malayan, and Central American.
417 Types of races—Terra del Fuegan, Negro, Bushman, Tasmanian.
     See also 262, 263 and 264.

(The Pilgrim's Progress—Part I.)
418 Pilgrim sets out from the City of Destruction.
419 Pilgrim meets Obstinate and Pliable.
420 The Slough of Despond.
421 Pilgrim meets Evangelist.
422 Pilgrim at the Wicket Gate.
423 At the Interpreter's—The Fire of Grace.
424 Ditto—The triumph of Resolution.
425 Christian at the Cross.
426 Simple, Sloth, and Presumption.
427 Christian asleep in the Arbour.
428 Christian and the Lions.
429 Christian at the Palace Beautiful.
430 Christian in Conflict with Apollyon.
431 The Giants Pope and Pagan.
432 Christian and Faithful at Vanity Fair.
433 Demas and the Hill Lucre.

11

12

DIAGRAM **(Hindostan and the Hindoos**—*continued).*

No. M 6 Self torture.
     77 The Suttee—Widow Burning.
     M 28 Death of Hindoos on the banks of Ganges.
     M 30 Itinerant Preaching.
     M 29 Christian Village.
     L M 10 Brahmin renouncing Caste.
     M 57 Hindoos addressed by Christian Teacher.
     M 31 Women bringing presents of ric e
     M 62 View of Delhi.
     W M 6 Tippoo's Mausoleum.
     W M 7 Palanquin Travelling.
     L M 16 Procession of Juggernauth.
     L M 17 Scene ou the Ganges.
     M 54 Hindoo School near Madras.
            See also Nos. 76 and 77

(LARGE MAP OF INDIA, QUADRUPLE SIZE, 8ft. BY 6ft.)
LARGE MAP OF THE WORLD, 10ft. BY 6ft.

(China and the Chinese.)
     M 68 Pekin from the North.
     M 69 Canton from the River.
     W M 34 Joss-house.
     L M 12 Hong-Kong and town of Victoria.
     W M 33 Street in Victoria (Hong-Kong)
     M 70 Tiger of War, Soldiers and Mandarin.
     M 18 Buddhist Priest at his Devotions.
     L M 13 Missionary Preaching in Buddhist Temple.
     M 64 Funeral Procession.
     M 65 Opium Smokers' Den.
     M 66 Wedding Ceremony.
     M 67 Tract Distribution.

(New Zealand and the New Zealanders.)
     M 71 Map of N. Zealand, with views of N. Plymouth and Wellington.
     M 72 Auckland.
     M 73 Dunedin, Otago.
     W M 44 Travelling in the Bush.
     M 9 Head of New Zealand Savage.
     W M 43 War Dance.
     M 32 War Canoes.
     M 10 Dead Chief Lying in State.
     M 33 Attack upon Missionaries.
     W M 45 Distribution of Scriptures.
     M 35 Dying Christian Chief.
     M 34 Missionary Meeting.

(Burmah—the Propagation of the Gospel Society's Missions.)
     M 86 Shevay Dagon Pagoda, Rangoon.
     87 Porch of ditto.
     88 Mission School, Mandalay.
     89 Clergy House, Mandalay.
     90 Native Gharries at Entrance of Burmese Pagoda.
     91 King's Palace, Mandalay.
     92 Pagoda at Amarapoora.
     93 Kyoung at Foot of Mandalay Hills.

(**The Melanesian Mission—Propagation of the Gospel Society.**)

DIAGRAM
No. M 94 Map of the Melanesian Group of Islands.
    95 Parsonage on Mota.
    96 Native Hut on Mota.
    97 The late Bishop Patteson's House, Chapel, &c.
    98 The College Buildings, St. John's, Auckland.

(**Missionary Subjects.**)

A variety of Diagrams and Pictures, in addition to the above, may also be had to illustrate the Missions of the " Church Missionary Society," the " London Missionary Society," and the " Wesleyan Missions."

In hand, a set on " HISTORY OF PITCAIRN ISLAND."

*** The Diagrams are 3 feet by 4 feet in area, or some multiple thereof; printed on cloth ; adapted for distant inspection, coloured for gas or candle-light, and are both durable and portable. Although arranged in sets, they may generally be obtained singly.

Single Diagrams—*i. e.*, having one number attached—are sold at 3s. each ; double, treble, and quadruple Diagrams in proportion. When required, they can be provided with frames and eyelets for convenient suspension.

The usual allowances to Subscribers to the Union and to the Trade. N.B. All transactions are for ready money.

WILLIAM THORN, Depositary,
28, Paternoster Row, London, E.C.

NOTE.—Detailed Lists forwarded on receipt of a Halfpenny Postage Stamp.